Making Model Buildings

Making Model Buildings

Stuart Dalby

BLANDFORD PRESS
Poole   Dorset

First published in the U.K. 1980

Copyright © 1980 Blandford Press Ltd,
Link House, West Street,
Poole, Dorset, BH15 1LL

British Library Cataloguing in Publication Data

Dalby, Stuart
   Making model buildings.
   1. Architectural models
   I. Title
   745.59'28   NA2790

ISBN 0 7137 0976 6

Set in 10/11pt Monophoto Optima and printed by
BAS Printers Limited, Over Wallop, Hampshire

Contents

This book is dedicated to my wife and children

Acknowledgements

I wish to thank the following for their help and advice while I was preparing this book.

The National Trust. Mrs Peggy Smith, custodian of Wordsworth House, and the staff for their patience. The Welsh Office. The Property Services Agency, Department of the Environment. Royal Commission on Ancient and Historical Monuments in Wales. The Librarian, United States Embassy, London. Wyoming State Archives and Historical Department. Fort Laramie National Historic Site. Mr Ralph Povey, The Keighley and Worth Valley Light Railway Limited. Pat, Christopher and Amanda for their patience and understanding.

Introduction

Making model buildings is a fascinating world, creating realism in miniature. It has perhaps, never been easier than today, when modern technology has produced a host of every day materials, which enable even the beginner to work with ease.

This book sets out to show you how to build five models. Each model is based on a famous building, one of which, the Globe Theatre, has passed into extinction. The buildings are not intended just as models, but are to be used in learning and play. Shakespeare's Globe becomes a living theatre, Wordsworth House a collector's dolls' house, while Oakworth Station is designed for the model railway enthusiast, just growing serious about his hobby.

Great skill and knowledge are not required, nor are expensive tools and materials.

The materials, specified for each model, are to standard sizes which are freely available at 'do-it-yourself' and model shops.

Construction has been made easy by the simplification of detail on the models. However, should you wish to add further detail a little research will make this easy to do. I hope you have as much fun making the models as I did. And I hope you will derive pleasure from their use.

Stuart Dalby, Stourbridge 1980

The measurements in this book are metric.
For the purposes of conversion; 10 mm = 1 cm.
1 cm = ⅜ in. 2 cm = ¾ in. 3 cm = 1⅛ in.
4 cm = 1⅝ in. 5 cm = 2 in.

1 The Globe Theatre

Before 1576 there were no permanent playhouses or theatres in England. Plays were mostly performed within the yards of inns, noblemen's houses, town halls or the royal palaces. In London the Lord Mayor and city aldermen were a constant hindrance to companies of actors. The gathering of crowds was seen as a danger to the community, an opportunity for petty crime.

Unhappy with this situation, James Burbage, a carpenter turned actor, then leader of the earl of Leicester's players, built a theatre outside the London city boundary. This first theatre was a great success and several more theatres were built by rival companies. The great playwrights of the time, Marlowe, Greene, Peele, Lodge and Shakespeare responded to the new opportunity with plays that today are classics of the English language.

In 1598, the two sons of James Burbage dismantled their father's theatre and moved it to Bankside on the South Bank of the Thames. They called this new theatre 'The Globe' after its emblem of Hercules carrying the world on his shoulders. The Globe was to be Shakespeare's theatre, where his troupe of actors performed the plays he had written. The Elizabethans loved sound effects and during a production of *Henry VIII* a small cannon, probably positioned in the turret, was fired setting alight the thatched roof. The theatre was burnt to the ground. Being wealthy, the company rebuilt their theatre within a year. This, the second Globe, no longer exists, having burnt down in 1613. Whilst there are neither plans nor detailed drawings regarding the construction of the first or second Globe Theatre, several writers and artists of the time have given us a good idea of its appearance. Almost certainly it echoed the atmosphere of the inn yards. These were circular in shape, with three tiers of galleries surrounding a yard or 'pit', a term taken from the bearbaiting arena. In Shakespeare's *Henry V* The Globe is referred to as 'this wooden O'.

The pit was open to the sky and we can imagine the 'groundlings', who occupied this area, having a rough time during bad weather. The afternoon performances were something of a noisy affair, with the actors having to match their wits against jibes and comments from the audience, as well as competing with the cries of the fruit sellers.

The stage jutted out into the yard, bringing the audience onto three sides and affording the actors a greater intimacy. Behind the stage was the 'tiring house' which was usually curtained off. Above the stage was a two-gabled roof, while below, doors on either side enabled actors to make entrances and exits. Entrance and exit was needed to begin and end a scene, as the stage itself was never curtained off and carried little in the way of props or scenery.

For upper scenes, such as Romeo's climb to Juliet's balcony, a gallery was positioned above the back of the main stage, its floor being the flat roof of the tiring house. The galleries on the right and left of the stage were reserved as gentlemen's rooms. The pillars and panelling in these rooms were probably more ornate and decorative than in the other galleries.

Hoisting machinery for the ascent or descent of actors was housed in the stage roof. On top of the roof was a turret. It was from here a flag was raised, followed by three trumpet blasts, to announce the start of a performance.

My model of the second Globe Theatre is a simplified version of how the real theatre must have looked. For easier construction, the pillars and panelling have been reduced to their basic form. To allow you to reach inside the model, the gabled roof, together with the two outer tiring house walls, has been designed as a lift-off unit. Those of you who are interested in the idea can put on a complete performance of a play, using pipe-cleaner figures as actors. The pipe-cleaners can be dressed with old fabrics and manipulated by wire rods from the open back of the tiring house. You can also change the scenery to suit the play, using card cut-outs placed at the back of the stage.

You will need

– the following tools

Drill with bits ranging from 1 mm to 5 mm
   drilling diameter plus a small countersink bit.
Fretsaw with fine blades.
Hand saw.
Small craft saw or junior hacksaw with fine
   blades.
Craft knife.
Hammer.
Screwdriver.
Vice and sawing block (optional).
Scissors, heavy duty.
Bradawl.
Metric ruler, preferably steel.
Carpenter's square, or set square.
Compasses.
Length of string, approximately 1 m long.
Small bulldog clips or clamps.

– the following materials

One piece of 12 mm plywood, 540 mm ×
   540 mm, for base of model.
Three pieces of 4 mm plywood, 460 mm ×
   460 mm, for floors for galleries, tiring house
   and roof base.
One piece of 4 mm plywood, 1500 mm ×
   167 mm, for outer walls.

One piece of 4 mm plywood, 312 mm × 150 mm,
   for gables of tiring house.
One piece of 4 mm plywood, 195 mm × 150 mm,
   for rear gables of tiring house.
2 mm plywood or card approximately 1 m ×
   1 m.
12 mm × 20 mm wood fillet approximately 2 m
   length.
12 mm × 12 mm wood fillet approximately 3 m
   length.
10 mm diameter dowel approximately 2.5 m
   length.
5 mm × 2 mm balsawood strip or card strip
   approximately 500 mm long.
5 mm × 5 mm balsawood fillet approximately
   500 mm long.
Small pieces of fabric for stage curtains and flag.
100 mm × 30 mm transparent acetate sheet for
   gable windows.
Self tapping countersink screws no. 1 size, 10 mm
   long.
Self tapping countersink screws no. 1 or 2 size,
   18 mm long.
25 mm veneer pins.
6 mm veneer pins.
Six sheets of coarse glasspaper.
Length of strong thread.
Plastic Padding or any other proprietary brand of
   wood/metal filler.
Impact adhesive.
Enamel paints from a model makers store.

Notes on materials

Because it is not easy to calculate the exact
requirements in size for every part of the model, sizes
have been rounded up. These rounded up sizes
represent the amounts of material I had at my
disposal when the model was started. All cutaway,
waste pieces were saved and used for smaller parts of
the model, so little in the way of left-overs remained
when the model was finished. Wood filleting tends to
be sold a little below or above the size that stores
advertise it at, this is due to cutting and planing during
production. The sizes given here are the exact sizes as
bought and although it is not essential for you to
follow these dimensions exactly, it is a good idea to
remember this point when buying your materials.

To begin your model

Mark out the model base

Take a piece of 12 mm thick plywood, 540 mm × 540 mm, and using a ruler join opposite corners so that the lines cross at the centre. Divide each side of the baseboard in half and join the opposite points together, forming two further lines. These lines should be horizontal and perpendicular to the edge facing you, and should also cross at the centre. Refer to baseboard layout diagram, figure 1.1.

You need to draw three circles on the baseboard to mark the positions for the outer wall edges, gallery seats, and pillars. To simplify this you will need to improvise your own compasses from a length of string and a veneer pin. The pin should be driven into the centre of the baseboard at a point where the lines cross. Tie a length of parcel string to the veneer pin, pull the string taut against the pin and make sure that it will revolve easily on its knot. Tie a short length of pencil to the other end of the string, making sure that its point forms a 230 mm radius from the pin

when the string is pulled tight.

Keeping the pencil upright and the string tight, draw the circle marked A on figure 1.1. Having completed this, draw the circles B and C, see figure 1.1.

The three circles need to be marked so that each circle can have sixteen sides drawn on it. Take an ordinary pair of compasses set at about 100 mm radius. Now refer to figure 1.1 and with the compass point at the first point d draw an arc. Put the compass point on the second d and draw a second arc that forms a cross at e. The point e should then be joined to the centre of the baseboard. Continue making arc points in the other seven segments of the circle. Join up the crossing points to the centre as before. Where each line cuts a circle a new point is formed. These new points should be joined up to form sixteen sided circles as in figure 1.2. Note that in figure 1.2, on lines B and C, parts of the sixteen sides (F) are not shown for obvious reasons.

Fig. 1.1   Baseboard layout.

Fig. 1.2   Fully drawn baseboard layout.

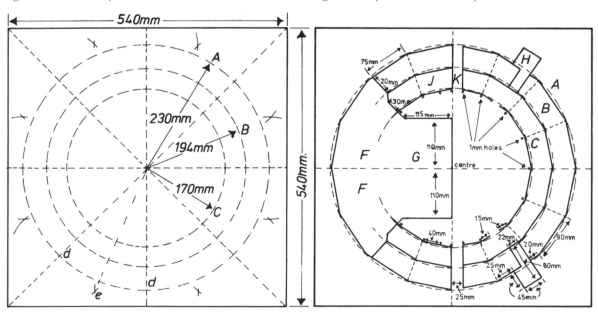

Using figure 1.2 as your guide, you can now go ahead and mark out the baseboard. On this diagram the area marked *F* is the tiring house position, *G* the stage area. *H* is the shape of the staircases, *J* the gentlemen's rooms and *K* the entrances. The dimensions are identical on each side of the centre line.

Refer to figure 1.2 again and drill holes on the baseboard at the hole-points on the circle marked *C*. These holes are to take the screws that will later fix the gallery pillars in place. Countersink the holes from the back of the baseboard and finish off with glasspaper.

Cut out the gallery floors

It is best to cut out the gallery floors, stage and tiring house floors in one operation before proceeding further with the model. The floors should be cut out of 4 mm plywood, figures 1.3 and 1.4 show the dimensions for these. You will notice that marking out is similar to the technique used earlier on the baseboard. In figure 1.3 the piece marked *L* is the first gallery floor. *F* and *G* are the stage and tiring house floor, which should be cut away from *L*, as shown in the diagram.

Figure 1.4 shows the second gallery floor *N* and the second tiring house floor and balcony *M*. Before cutting these out it is a good idea to trace the shape of *M* onto tracing paper, and transfer this to another piece of 4 mm plywood. You will then be able to cut out the top tiring house floor, which should be minus the balcony protrusion.

Note that the broken lines in figures 1.3 and 1.4 represent your construction lines and the position of seats and panelling, while the shaded portions represent the areas to be cut away. When all these pieces have been cut out, they should be checked against the baseboard layout to make sure that the pieces match, or fit, within their appropriate areas. Remember that the first and second gallery floors overlap each other on the inner pillar circle, position *C* in figure 1.2.

Outer walls and staircase

Refer to figures 1.5 to 1.9 and cut these out of 4 mm plywood. The number of pieces required is stated in the caption to each diagram. Shaded areas should be cut away with a fretsaw or a craftknife. The broken lines represent your pencil lines for floor and roof base positions. Remember to clean up around the door openings with a piece of fine glasspaper wrapped around a wood fillet.

Fig. 1.3   Tiring house, stage and first gallery floor.

Fig. 1.4   Second floor tiring house and second gallery.

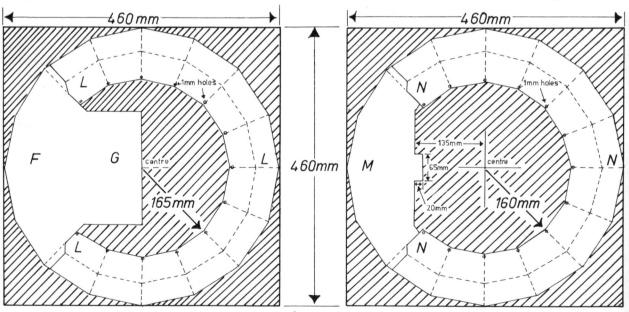

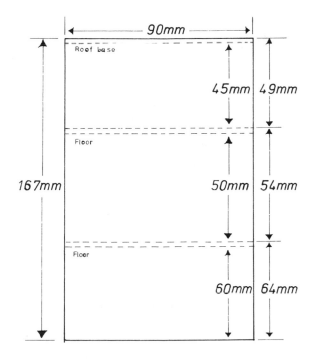

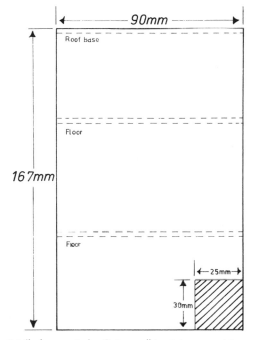

Fig. 1.8 (below centre)   Outer wall to staircase: cut two.

Fig. 1.9 (below right)   Side wall to staircase: cut four.

Fig. 1.5   Outer wall: cut twelve.

Fig. 1.6 (top right)   Entrance, outer wall: cut two.

Fig. 1.7   Inner wall to staircase: cut two.

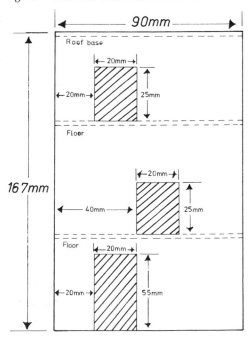

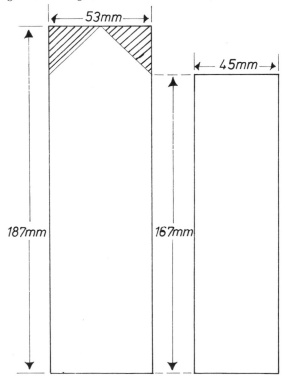

been marked out. The fillets should be fixed to the baseboard with adhesive and veneer pins. This outer ring of fillets supports the exterior walls of the theatre, as well as forming the back seat of the base gallery.

Seats

A cross-section of the base gallery seats is shown in figure 1.10. The seats are made from 12 mm × 12 mm wood fillet marked out and angled in the same way as the wall supports, see above. It is best to complete the centre line of seats, which needs to be jacked up with

Outer wall supports and seat backs on base

Seat construction on marked out theatre base. Notice the sliver of wood jacking up the centre line of seats.

You can now turn your attention to building up the seats on the baseboard. Using 20 mm × 12 mm wood filleting, cut lengths of 90 mm. Figure 1.10a shows how each 90 mm length is positioned on the baseboard, for marking out the angles for cutting with a craft saw. Note that the line marked A in figure 1.10a corresponds to the outer circle A marked on figure 1.2. You will find it easiest to cut one fillet at a time and fix it in place once its adjoining pieces have

a 5 mm wood sliver, before moving on to the other seats.

Gentlemen's rooms on the base

The seating arrangement of the gentlemen's rooms differs from the rest of the base gallery. There are only two seats. These are made from 12 mm × 12 mm

Completed seats and stage support. The panels of the gentlemen's rooms are mounted with a spacer behind them.

Fig. 1.10   Cross-section of seats on base.

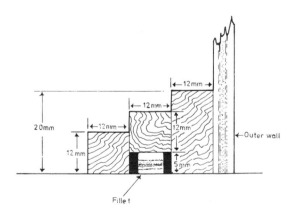

Fig. 1.10a   Marking out the angles for the seats.

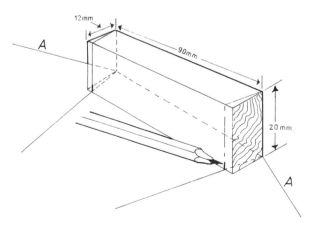

filleting and butt up to the panelling. Behind the panelling is a 20 mm × 12 mm spacer between the panelling and the outer wall support. Figure 1.11 shows a cross-section of this. You will need to cut out the panels shown in 11a and 11b and the spacers, which must be small blocks. Before fixing these in place, position the panels and spacers on the baseboard. Mark the width of the door opening in figure 1.11b on the baseboard, this will give you the width of your steps from the entrance wall line. Fix the spacers and panelling in place before building up the seats as shown in figure 1.11. Repeat this procedure for the opposite side of the theatre base.

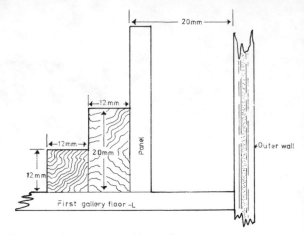

Fig. 1.12   Cross-section of first gallery.

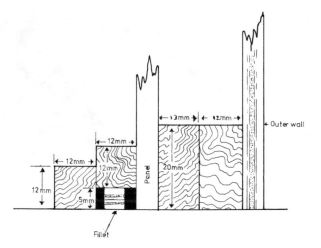

Fig. 1.11   Cross-section of seats, gentlemen's rooms on base.

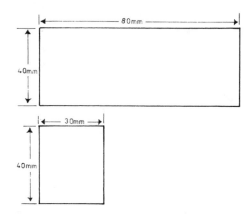

Fig. 1.12a (above)   Panel for first gallery.

Fig. 1.12b (middle)   Seat dividing panel, gentlemen's rooms first gallery.

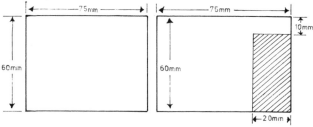

Fig. 1.11a (left)   Panel for gentlemen's rooms, stage side on base.

Fig. 1.11b (right)   Panel for gentlemen's rooms, entrance side on base.

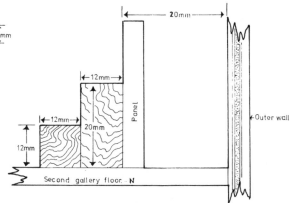

Fig. 1.13   Cross-section of second gallery.

16

The base gallery; stage and outer walls assembled before painting. The entrance panels are in position.

Entrance panels

Figure 1.14 shows a panel for gentlemen's rooms side of main entrance. These will need to be fixed to the side of the stair block on base gallery. Figure 1.15 shows a panel for public gallery side of main entrance. This panel should be glued to the end of the stairs in public gallery, leaving an entrance space in front. Repeat this instruction for each main entrance. Fix in place once the stairs have been made and mounted.

Fig. 1.13a (left)   Panel for second gallery.

Fig. 1.13b (left centre)   Seat dividing panel, gentlemen's rooms second gallery.

Fig. 1.14 (right centre)   Main entrance panel, gentlemen's rooms side.

Fig. 1.15 (right)   Main entrance panel, public side.

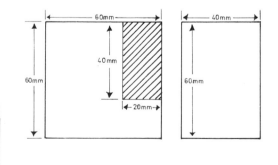

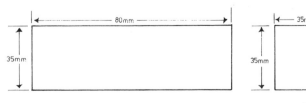

Stairs

There are four sets of stairs to be made for the theatre base. The sets leading up between the seats in the public gallery give access to the staircases which will later protrude outwards on either side of the theatre. These staircases allowed the wealthier to reach their seats in the first and second galleries. The other two sets of stairs were positioned in the gentlemen's rooms, and probably allowed access to the tiring house. The stairs to the public gallery are made from three lengths of 20 mm × 12 mm filleting, precut and stacked one on top of the other. Figure 1.16 shows how this is done. The stairs to the gentlemen's rooms are made from two lengths of filleting. Figures 1.17 and 1.18 show the stairs in cross-section. The shaded areas should be cut out with a finesaw.

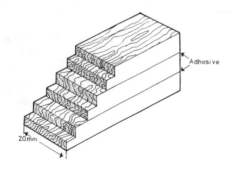

Fig. 1.16 (above)   Stair block assembly.

Fig. 1.17 (below left)   Cross-section of stairs to public staircases.

Fig. 1.18 (below right)   Cross-section of stairs to gentlemen's rooms.

Having glued the precut fillets together, so that they form a stair block, fix them in place on the baseboard. The public gallery stairs fit within the lines drawn at H and the stairs in the gentlemen's rooms are fixed with one side on the entrance line K, both in figure 1.2.

Stage floor support-fillet

To support the stage floor (which you have already prepared) cut 20 mm × 12 mm wood filleting and fix it along the line which borders areas F and G in figure 1.2. Perfect corner mitres are not essential as they will be covered later, but it is best to follow the same procedures for marking out and fixing as were employed for the wall supports.

Having done this, you can now fix the stage floor to the supports. Some trimming may be needed around the edge of the floor where it meets the panels of the gentlemen's rooms.

Pillars

Cut fifteen gallery pillars as shown in figure 1.20 and two entrance posts as shown in figure 1.19. Drill a fine guide hole into the centre of one end of each pillar. Using adhesive to keep them in place, fix the pillars to the base with screws passed through the holes previously drilled on circle C in the baseboard. Make sure that you keep the pillars perpendicular to the base. The entrance posts are fixed one to each end of the public gallery.

Cut an 18 mm wide strip of 2 mm card or plywood and measure the distance between the pillars. Cut a strip to fit between the two pillars and use this strip as a template for the rest. These are the barriers around the base gallery. You will need to leave spaces in the barrier for the stair entrances to the public galleries, and to the gentlemen's rooms, see figure 1.2. Now fix the entrance panels.

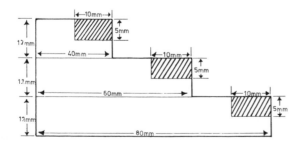

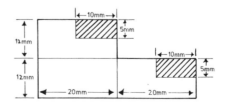

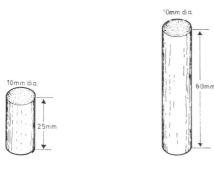

Fixing the outer walls

The outer walls should now be fixed to the wall supports. Use veneer pins and adhesive. As you fix each one make sure that it is square to the base before passing on to the next. The staircase inner walls will slot in place over the stair blocks, see figure 1.7. Do not fix the last two walls to the tiring house as these must be fixed to the gabled roof so that they can be lifted away.

Staircases

To make a staircase, glue the edges of two side walls, figure 1.9, to the inner face of one gabled wall, figure 1.8. Now glue the staircase in place, area *H* in figure 1.2.

Fig. 1.19 (left)   Main entrance post: cut two.

Fig. 1.20 (right)   Gallery pillar on base: cut fifteen.

Outer walls and one staircase fixed to the base. The two tiring house walls will be attached to the roof section.

Painting

The inside of the theatre, as far as completed, should be painted before the first floor gallery is fixed in position. Paint the base gallery walls light brown, the seats grey-brown and the floor green-brown. Panelling and pillars should be painted a deep red-brown.

View into the theatre, showing the textured floor of the pit area.

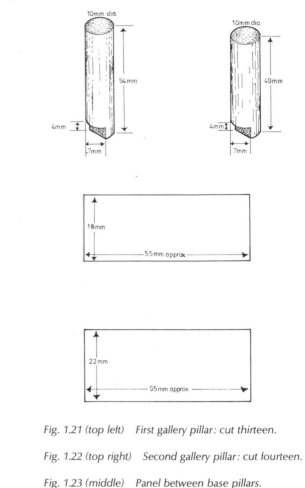

Fig. 1.21 (top left)   First gallery pillar: cut thirteen.

Fig. 1.22 (top right)   Second gallery pillar: cut fourteen.

Fig. 1.23 (middle)   Panel between base pillars.

Fig. 1.24 (bottom)   Panel for between pillars, first and second gallery.

To add realistic texture to the theatre floor, cover the pit area with a coarse grade of glasspaper. Make a tracing paper template of the pit area. This will help you cut the glasspaper to shape. Where you need to overlap the sheets of glasspaper make the edges jagged to disguise the join. Fix the glasspaper to the baseboard with adhesive and score the surface with a nail to give added effect. In the real Globe the pit was just that, soil and sand with no floorboards.

First gallery pillars

You will need to cut thirteen pillars, see figure 1.21. Each pillar has a notch cut into its base end. This notch overlaps the gallery base before being fixed in place with screws and adhesive. Pillar panels to go between the pillars are made from 2 mm thick card, see figure 1.24.

When you have finished the first gallery paint it as you did the base gallery, before fixing it into place over the pillars and panel edges of the base gallery.

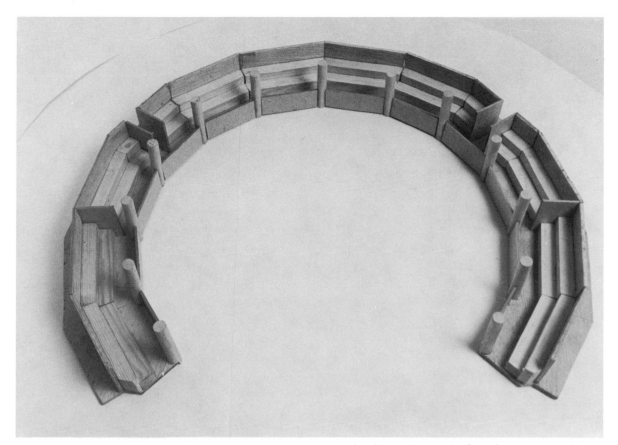

Completed first gallery. Notice how the gentlemen's rooms are divided with card panels slotted between the seats.

First gallery

This is constructed separately from the main part of the model, on a 4 mm thick plywood base, area *L* figure 1.3. The diagram of area *L* shows the seat lines depicted by dashes. Figure 1.12 shows a cross-section of the seat construction. Carry this out as you did for the base gallery. Figure 1.12a shows the panels for the seat backs. Cut ten of these. You will also need smaller panels on either side of the passage ways to the stairs. Cut these panels from 2 mm thick card or plywood. Panels for dividing up the gentlemen's rooms are shown in figure 1.12b.

Second gallery

Following the portion of the diagram marked *N* in figure 1.4, and the cross-section diagram in figure 1.13, construct the second gallery as you did the first. Note the change in position of the entrance from the staircase. Paint and fix in place over first gallery.

All the galleries fixed in place. The roof base supports are fixed to the inner side of the theatre walls—see section on roof base.

Finishing the outer side of theatre walls

You will need to fill the gap between each of the meeting edges of each of the fourteen outer walls. Use a resin or plastic based filler to do this and sand smooth when dry. Trim the edges of the main entrances with match sticks.

Tiring house floors

There are two floors, each mounted at gallery levels, above the tiring house floor. These floors are supported by the gallery end panels, check with figure 1.25. Take the two tiring house floors that you cut from 4 mm plywood, area M in figure 1.4, and make sure they slot neatly between the gallery ends and the outer walls of the tiring house. Now turn to figure 1.25 and cut nine panels from 2 mm card. Lay

them out as shown. Cut another set of these panels to fit the other side of the tiring house. These separate the galleries from the tiring house. Starting with the row of panels at the bottom of the diagram, glue the bottom edge of X to the base gallery floor, and glue an upright edge to the inside of the theatre wall. Panel Y is glued to the narrow angle formed by the end of the base gallery seat backs. Panel Z is glued along the gallery edge finishing at the pillar. Repeat this procedure on the opposite side of the tiring house, using the second set of panels.

The first tiring house floor, which has the balcony protrusion, is now glued into its position over these panels. This procedure is repeated for the middle and top line of panels. You may find it easier to paint each set of panels and the floor before constructing the level above.

Balcony

The balcony protrusion needs to be supported by the two dowel pillars shown in figure 1.26. The details for making the balcony hand rails are also shown in figure 1.26. Paint the rails gold. A foot rail can be added to the edge of the stage at the same height as the balcony hand rail. Use balsawood strips for this operation.

Make two curtains to fold over a piece of thick thread stretched between the balcony pillars.

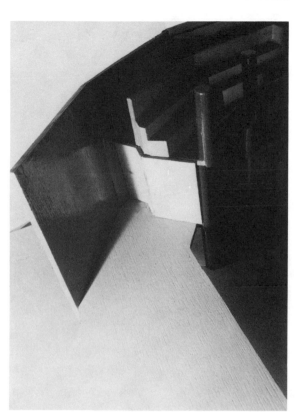

First tiring house floor in place. The end panels are ready to receive the top tiring house floor.

Fig. 1.25 (left)   The panels between the galleries and tiring house act as tiring house floor support.

Fig. 1.26 (right)   Dowel pillars and balcony protrusion.

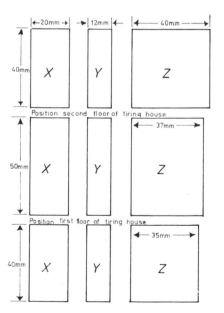

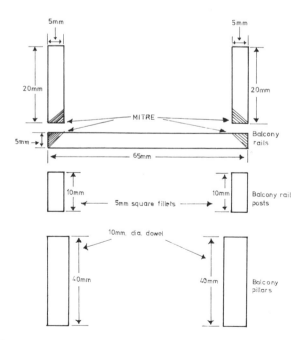

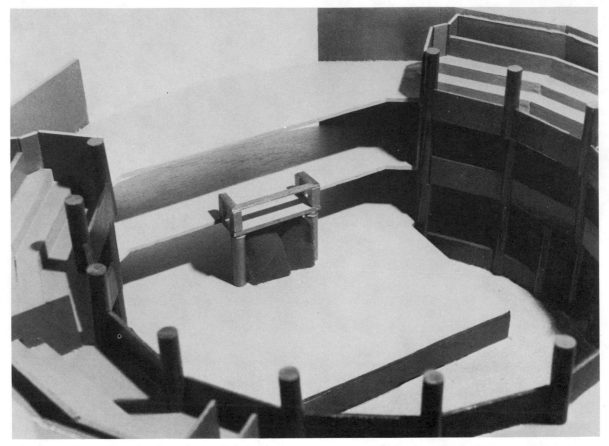

Both tiring house floors in place. The handrails for the balcony protrusion are made from balsawood fillet, with dowel for pillars.

Scenery

As explained in the introduction, the scenery can be to your own design. You will need one piece of 2 mm thick card 195 mm × 140 mm and two side panel pieces 140 mm × 25 mm. Figure 1.27 shows a suggested scene design for Romeo and Juliet. The squared up area, at the top of the diagram, is to help you draw the scrolls. Each square represents 5 mm × 5 mm and you should draw these onto your scene card before attempting to copy the scroll work.

All shaded areas should be cut out. The broken lines represent your pencil lines. Paint the scenery in brilliant colours. Curtains should be hung from the back of the scenery so that they cover the scenery windows and the space behind the scenery balcony. Elastic bands stretched between two screws will make

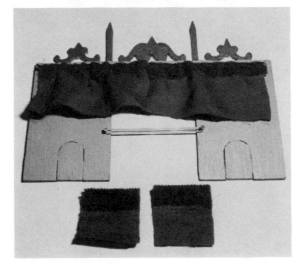

The back of the scenery before slotting in place. The curtains are draped from an elastic band stretched between the screws. Doors have been fixed in their openings.

24

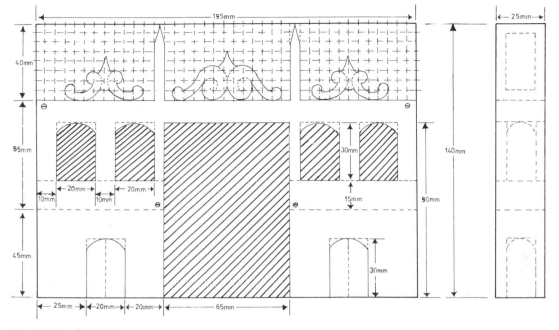

Fig. 1.27 Scenery for stage.

this easy. The screw positions are shown in figure 1.27. You will need to slip the scenery over the balcony, before hanging the curtains. Glue the scenery to the edge of the tiring house floors and then add the side panels. You will find it easier to change the scenery if you use only small blobs of glue.

Roof base

The roof base, figure 1.28, is made from 4 mm plywood and is identical in shape to the gallery floors. It will need supporting around the inside of the theatre walls. Cut ten pieces of 2 mm thick card, 90 mm × 45 mm, and glue these cards to the theatre walls, the bottom edge of each card in contact with the second gallery floor. Paint these cardboard supports light brown. The staircase wall will not need one of these supports. When you have completed this, place the roof base in position and check that it fits flush with the top edge of the theatre walls.

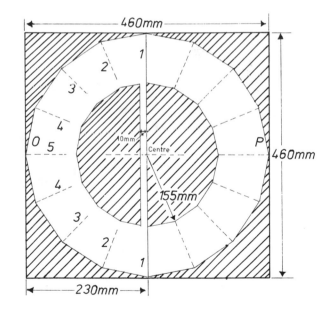

Fig. 1.28 Roof bases O and P.

25

Slotting the scenery into place.

Theatre roof

Roof base P in position with roof supports in place.

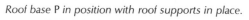

The theatre roof is made in two halves. One half is fixed over the gallery section, while the other half slots over the tiring house and the pit. You should make the fixed roof first.

Refer to figure 1.28 and cut the roof base from 4 mm plywood. Semi circle *P* should be cut away from semi circle *O* down the right-hand edge of the centre line. Having checked that it fits, glue semi circle *P* in position over the gallery area directly opposite the stage and tiring house. Take further pieces of 4 mm plywood and cut out nine roof supports, these are shown in figure 1.30. These roof supports should be glued along the sectional lines of the roof base, shown as the broken lines on semi circle *P* figure 1.28. Note that the inner edges of the roof supports face into the theatre centre, and that all the supports should overlap the roof base on the inside and outside edges.

The actual roof pieces are made from 2 mm thick plywood or card. Start to cover the outer side of the roof supports first. Figure 1.31 shows a roof piece. It should be fixed between two roof supports so that it reaches half way across each roof support edge. Make

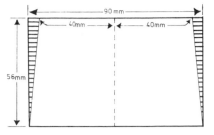

Fig. 1.31   Outer roof panel to base piece P.

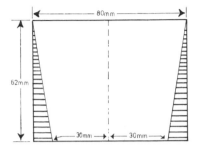

Fig. 1.32   Inner roof panel to base piece P.

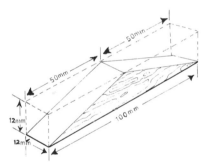

Fig. 1.29   Brace made from filleting.

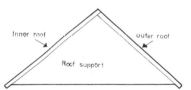

Fig. 1.33   Roof support.

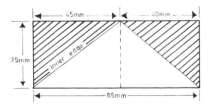

Fig. 1.30   Roof support, base piece P: cut nine.

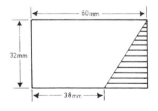

Fig. 1.34   Staircase roof: cut four.

a card template of figure 1.31 and use this to check each roof piece before cutting out the next one and gluing it in place. Note that the outer pieces should fit flush with the apex of the roof supports, while the inner pieces should cover this, see figure 1.33. Having covered the outer roof sections on base P, you can cover the inner sections using pieces made to the dimensions given in figure 1.32.

To cover the staircase roofs you will need to cut four pieces of 2 mm card to the shape shown in figure 1.34. Glue these in position to the staircase gables and theatre roof.

Before building the roof on roof base O, you should fix the remaining two outer theatre walls to the underside of the roof base. These outer walls must be glued to two 20 mm × 12 mm fillets, 90 mm in length, fixed 4 mm away from the two edges shown either side of the broken line 5 on figure 1.28. To support these walls further, make the brace shown in figure 1.29. Glue this brace to the centre of the inner side of the walls. Turn the base O together with the two attached walls, top side up and slot in place over the tiring house and gentlemen's rooms.

The roof supports to roof base O vary in size. This is to achieve the required roof sweep for this section. Look at the diagrams in figure 1.35 and using 4 mm plywood cut out the number of pieces indicated. Each support is numbered to correspond with its numbered position in figure 1.28. Glue these supports in place on O with their outer edges facing out of the theatre.

Cover the outer side of the roof in the same manner as you covered the outer roof of base P. To find the shapes and sizes of the inner roof section, you will need to cut a card template roughly the size and shape of the template used for the inner roof sections of P. Lay this in place and mark off the shape of the first section. Cut this. Take the next measurement with the template and use it to cut your next roof section. Carry on all the way round the inner roof section until complete. You will need to tap two veneer pins into the roof base O. Each pin to go just in front of where the base meets the supports numbered 2. The pins will help to bend the roof section into place on the support.

Fig. 1.35   Roof supports to roof base O (tiring house).

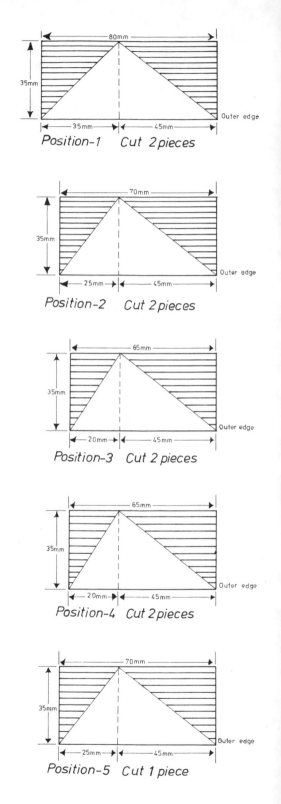

Position-1   Cut 2 pieces

Position-2   Cut 2 pieces

Position-3   Cut 2 pieces

Position-4   Cut 2 pieces

Position-5   Cut 1 piece

Roofing the inner side of the removable gabled roof section. Veneer pins are driven into O, to hold the first roof sections in place. The gable roof sides later bend over these pins.

Gabled roof

Cut the front and rear gable pieces from 4 mm plywood, see figures 1.36 and 1.37. Windows for the front gables should be made from transparent acetate sheet. The window frames and lattice work can be ruled on in black enamel, see figure 1.48. Glue the windows to the inside of the gables and use small pieces of fillet to make the window ledges. Paint the gables white, and paint on brown or black timbers.

The front gables are now glued to the cross beam which is part of base O and spans the stage. The rear gables glue in place on base O between the positions 4 and 3 on either side of 5, check figure 1.28. The inside joins of the gable pieces should be strengthened with 5 mm × 5 mm balsawood fillets.

Next cut the two centre roof pieces from 2 mm plywood or card, see figures 1.38 and 1.39. Glue these front and rear to the central **V** in the gables leaving an overlap at the front and rear. Note that the roof piece in figure 1.38 fits into place first.

*Roof gables fixed in place. Notice 5 mm × 5 mm balsawood supports behind gable walls; these strengthen section. The underside overhangs of roof, for central **V** of gables, have been painted before positioning.*

29

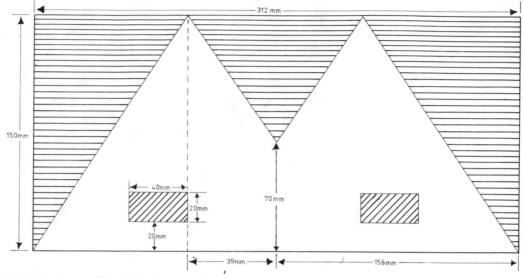

Fig. 1.36   Front gable of tiring house roof.

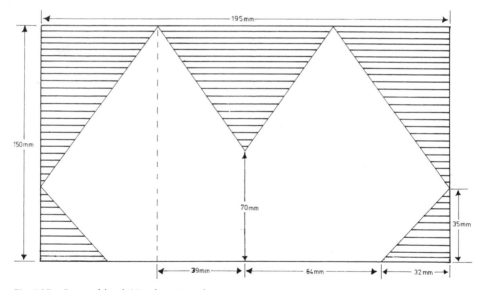

Fig. 1.37   Rear gable of tiring house roof.

Now turn to figure 1.40 which shows a gable side roof and cut two side roof pieces from 2 mm plywood. Score the underside of each piece several times with a craft knife to help the plywood bend. Using impact adhesive fix both side roof pieces to the gables. Do not attempt to bend the roof right back to the rear gable edge. Just tack it in place and leave it to shape for several hours. You will then find that the roof will bend

*Fig. 1.38 and Fig. 1.39 (opposite top & middle)   The two roof pieces for the central **V** of the gabled roof.*

Fig. 1.40 (opposite bottom)   A gable side roof: cut two.

fully back to the rear gable edge where you can fix it in place with small veneer pins.

To finish, paint the entire roof area tile red. For extra realism paint tile lines onto the roof.

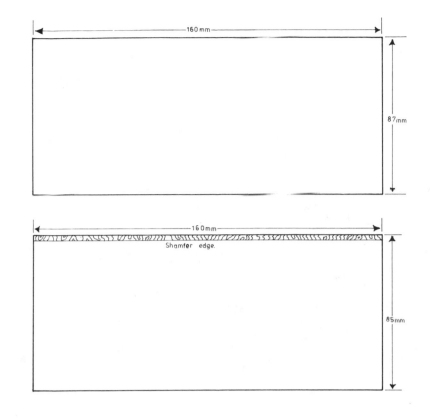

Shamfer edge.

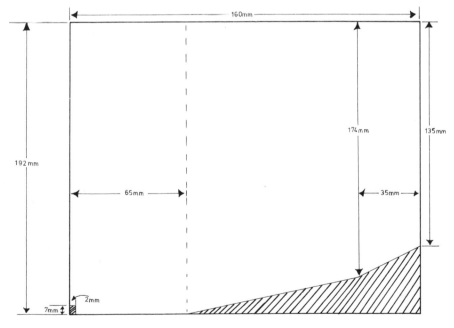

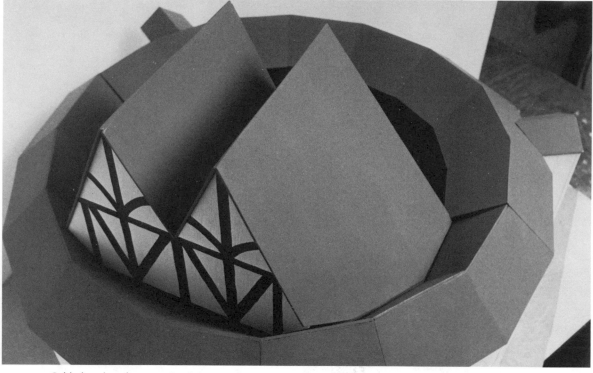

Gabled roof ready to receive the turret.

*When completed, the turret is glued into position 5 mm from the outer edge of the **V** of the gabled roof.*

Making the turret

Cut out the pieces in figures 1.41 and 1.42. Use 4 mm plywood. Cut the turret floor from 2 mm plywood, figure 1.43. Assemble by gluing the two side pieces in figure 1.42 inside the edges of the two pieces in figure 1.41. Incorporate the floor as you do this so that the turret forms a square.

The turret roof is made from four pieces of 2 mm card, figure 1.44. These are glued edge to edge to form a conical shape. The flagpole is made from a 200 mm length of 6 mm dowel tapered at one end. Drill a small hole into the tapered end to take the flag hoisting thread. Supports for the flag pole are shown in figures 1.45 and 1.46. The supports are made from card, one should be glued just above the outer window arches of figure 1.41, with the other support directly in line below the window ledge level. Paint the window portions and the interior of the turret light

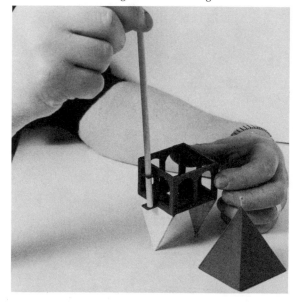

32

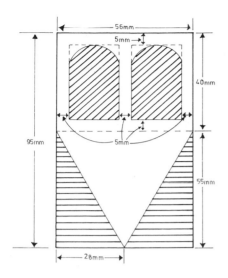

Fig. 1.41   Turret wall: cut two.

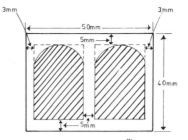
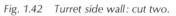

Fig. 1.42   Turret side wall: cut two.

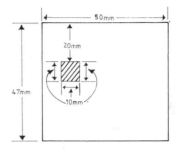

Fig. 1.43   Turret floor.

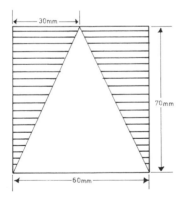

Fig. 1.44   Turret roof: cut four.

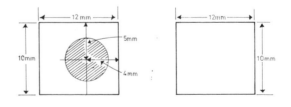

Fig. 1.45 (left)   Top flagpole support: drill 6 mm hole.

Fig. 1.46 (right)   Bottom flagpole support.

brown. Paint the two lower triangular sections white with brown or black timbers. Paint the roof, tile-red and finish off with a knob-headed map pin at the apex, painted gold. Glue the roof to the window section edges.

Mount the turret in place about 5 mm in from the outside edge of the roof.

As there are many windows around the outside walls of the theatre, you will find it easier to paint them if you make the template shown in figure 1.47. Place the bottom edge on the base and press the template against one wall section at a time, running a pencil

around the inside edges of each window. This will save you time. Paint the windows a medium grey. For added realism you can detail the windows with a lattice work effect.

The flag can be made from a small piece of fabric, the dimensions are given in figure 1.49. No information exists about the flag's original colour, but the one on my model was made from blue rayon with a gold circle or globe painted in the centre. To hoist, fold one edge of the flag and glue it over a length of thread. Pass the thread through the hole drilled in the top end of the flagpole. Run up the flag and tie the ends of the thread to one of the flag supports.

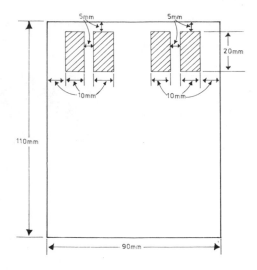

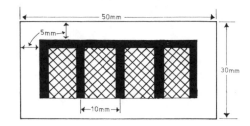

Fig. 1.48   Window for tiring house gables: make two.

Fig. 1.47   Template for windows on outer walls.

Fig. 1.49   The flag for The Globe.

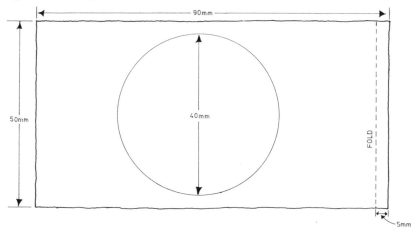

Using a template to mark out the windows on the outer walls.

Removing the roof to start a performance.

2 Wordsworth House

In 1745 Joshua Lucock, Sheriff of Cumberland, built a fine Georgian house in the Lake District town of Cockermouth. Its design was simple and neat, with windows set in moulded architraves and, over the front entrance, a porch of stone supported by Doric columns. To the rear of the house, gardens walled with local stone touched the bank of the River Derwent. Across the river were grazing pastures and open fields belonging to the property.

Some years later it passed into the ownership of the Lowther family. Sir James Lowther, later first earl of Lonsdale, let the house to John Wordsworth his agent and attorney-at-law.

It was here, in 1770, that William Wordsworth was born. An event to which the house now owes its fame. Wordsworth, the famous Lakeland poet, wrote in one of his poems that he was, 'much favoured in his birthplace'.

His mother died when he was eight, but in his early childhood she gave him freedom to play in the open air and encouraged his deep interest in nature. To him the River Derwent became the 'fairest of all rivers' and the fields beyond it a place of adventure and learning.

William's father built up a fine library of books, and he gave the boy a wide knowledge of great literature. John Wordsworth died when the boy was thirteen and William was placed under the guardianship of his uncles. Four years later, at the age of seventeen, he was sent to St John's Cambridge, the college where his mother's brother had been a fellow.

When I arrived at the house on a warm sunny day in August, its white stonework was bright with signs of constant upkeep. Having passed through the large entrance gates, I crossed a flagstone path and climbed the wide stone steps. Inside the porch two large panelled doors opened into a flagstone hallway. Two doors faced each other across the hallway and two pillars framed the area beyond.

Through the door on the left was the panelled morning room with its corner hob-grate fireplace. The right-hand door in the hallway opened into a larger sitting room with a magnificent Adam fireplace. Once again the room was walled with large fielded panels and floored in polished wood. The pillars at the end of the hallway led through to the staircase. To the right of the first step of the staircase was a door which led into two small adjoining rooms at the back of the house. The kitchen was reached across the flagstones to the left of the stairs. A door led from the kitchen to the dining room which was situated at the front left corner of the house. Directly before the kitchen door, the flagstones led to steps which ran along the side of the kitchen wall to a door at the rear of the house.

The stairs were balustraded and a magnificent window above the half-landing looked out over the rear gardens and the River Derwent. At the top of the staircase a large L shaped landing gave access to several rooms. The layout of the upper rooms was almost identical to those downstairs. To the left there were two doors. One led to two smaller back rooms. The other led to the drawing room which was as impressive as the sitting room beneath it. An interesting feature of the drawing room was the false door set into the far wall of the room. This was a fashionable trick of the mid-Georgian style.

A small dressing room, set between the drawing room and the bedrooms, spanned the width of space taken up by the hallway beneath it. A door within the dressing room gave access to the two bedrooms at the front of the house.

A corridor led through an arch to the right of the stairs and stretched along to the kitchen end of the house. The rear bedroom and the front corner bedroom were entered from this corridor.

The house had well proportioned cornices. Every door was panelled and painted white and had brass door-furniture.

Space does not permit me to include details of the gardens at the front and rear, or the small stables joining the right-hand side of the house.

My model of Wordsworth House is a simplified version of the actual building. To achieve this simplicity, complete accuracy of detail has not been possible. This model will, however, provide you with a good impression of the real Wordsworth House. My model has been designed to open at front and rear so that it can be used as a dolls' house. The roof lifts off to reveal the top floor interior.

Furniture and fittings can be devised to equip the house in Georgian style. You yourself can probably find ways to add further detail.

You will need

– the following tools

Drill with bits ranging from 1 mm to 5 mm diameter plus a countersink bit.
Fretsaw or jigsaw attachment.
Hand saw.
Small craft saw or junior hacksaw.
Craft knife with spare blades.
Scissors.
Hammer.
Small screwdriver.
Vice and sawing block (optional)
Bradawl.
Mitre block or similar tool.
Metric ruler, preferably steel.
Carpenter's square or set square.
Compasses.
Artist's brushes, small.
Larger painting brushes.

– the following materials

One piece of 12 mm plywood, 900 mm × 570 mm, for base of model
Two pieces of 12 mm plywood, 400 mm × 400 mm, for exterior side walls.
One piece of 12 mm plywood, 836 mm × 400 mm, for upper interior floor.
One piece of 12 mm plywood, 836 mm × 170 mm, for interior wall A.
One piece of 12 mm plywood, 400 mm × 170 mm, for interior wall B.
Two pieces of 12 mm plywood, 200 mm × 170 mm, for interior walls C and E.
Two pieces of 12 mm plywood, 188 mm × 170 mm, for interior walls D and F.
One piece of 12 mm plywood, 350 mm × 188 mm, for interior wall G.
One piece of 12 mm plywood, 400 mm × 166 mm, for interior wall J.
One piece of 12 mm plywood, 354 × 166 mm, for interior wall K.
One piece of 12 mm plywood, 188 mm × 166 mm, for interior wall L.
One piece of 12 mm plywood, 166 mm × 100 mm, for interior wall M.

Two pieces of 12 mm plywood, 200 mm × 166 mm, for interior walls N and O.
One piece of 12 mm plywood, 370 mm × 166 mm, for interior wall P.
One piece of 12 mm plywood, 282 mm × 166 mm, for interior wall Q.
Two pieces of 12 mm plywood, 870 mm × 399 mm, for exterior walls.
Two pieces of 12 mm plywood, 836 mm × 45 mm, ground floor supports.
One piece of 6 mm plywood, 836 mm × 400 mm, for ground floor.
One piece of 6 mm plywood, 880 mm × 420 mm, for roof base.
One piece of 6 mm plywood, 880 mm × 150 mm, for roof piece U.
One piece of 6 mm plywood, 870 mm × 140 mm, for roof piece V.
Two pieces of 6 mm plywood, 445 mm × 180 mm, for roof pieces W.
Four pieces of 6 mm plywood, 335 mm × 170 mm, for roof pieces X.
Various offcuts of 6 mm plywood for stairs etc.
One Imperial size or A2 size mounting board (or card), grey on one side.
One piece of clear acetate sheet from a craft shop, about 500 mm linear size.
One sheet of white cartridge paper.
Three 1 m lengths of 5 mm × 2 mm wood fillet.
1 m of 10 mm × 10 mm wood fillet.
2 m of concave quadrant beading.
5 m of 20 mm × 10 mm wood fillet.
1 m of 15 mm dowel.
Length of 6 mm diameter plastic or rubber tube.
Thirty small brass upholstery nails, collar studs or paper fasteners.
Self tapping screws no. 1 or 2 size, 10 mm and 18 mm long.
25 mm veneer pins.
6 mm veneer pins.
Glasspaper.
Impact adhesive.
Plastic Padding or similar metal/wood filler.
Enamel paints as required.
Clear varnish.
Hinges.

To begin your model

Mark out the base

The base of the house is made from a sheet of 12 mm plywood measuring 900 mm × 570 mm. Figure 2.1 shows how this is marked out to receive the exterior side walls and ground floor supports. The broken line represents the 45 mm deep supports cut from 12 mm plywood. The thick solid lines on either side are the side walls. The 150 mm gap at the bottom of the diagram will be the front of the house. Drill holes at the wall and support positions to take 15 mm no. 1 size screws. Countersink these holes from the reverse of the base.

Before fixing any pieces to the base, it is a good idea

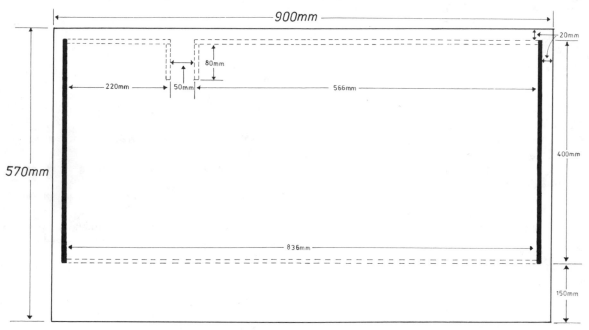

Fig. 2.1   Baseboard layout.

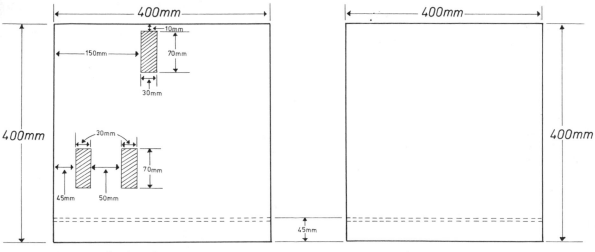

Fig. 2.2   Left side wall.   Fig. 2.3   Right side wall.

Ground floor with walls in place, seen from the front. The fireplace was bought from a modelling shop and was adapted to fit the model.

to edge the base with 20 mm × 10 mm wood fillet.

Using figures 2.2 and 2.3 as your guide, cut the exterior side walls from 12 mm plywood. The shaded areas in figure 2.2 are the two kitchen windows and the upper floor corridor window. The broken lines indicate where 10 mm × 10 mm fillet should be fixed to the inside of each piece. This fillet lies level with the ground floor supports when the sides are screwed to the base. This means that when in place, the ground floor is supported at both sides as well as at the front and back.

Fix the ground floor supports to the base, followed by the side walls. Figure 2.2 is fixed to the left of the base, with the kitchen windows nearest the rear of the house.

The ground floor

A piece of 6 mm plywood, 836 mm × 400 mm, is used for the ground floor. Refer to figure 2.4 and mark out as shown. The shaded area represents the opening that takes the steps from the rear entrance. The broken lines are the positions that the interior walls will take when they are screwed onto the ground floor.

Having marked out the floor and cut away all waste, lightly glasspaper the edges at the front and rear. You are now ready to score in the floorboard pattern and print the flat stone effect. Start by scoring the floorboard pattern, having placed the plywood flat on a sound working surface. Each floorboard line should be spaced 10 mm from the one before and should run from the front to rear of the floor area. Do not score the floorboard lines on the areas intended for the kitchen, rear passage, staircase or hallway. In the diagram the kitchen is bound by the lines A and F. The rear passage by the lines F, A and G. The staircase area is bound by G, A and B. The hallway by the lines C, A and B.

First mark out the floorboard lines in pencil. Then, using a steel ruler and a craft knife, score the lines about ½ mm into the plywood surface. When finished rub down with fine glasspaper and coat with clear varnish.

For the flagstone area use grey enamel paint from a

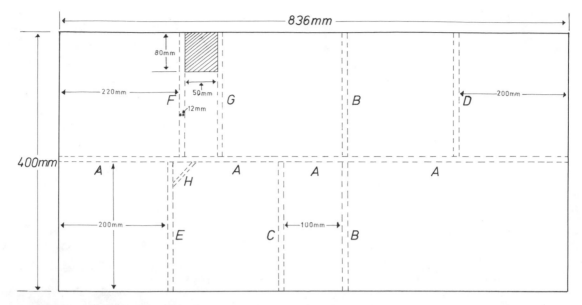

Fig. 2.4 Ground floor layout and base.

Printing the flagstone effect. Use a brush to apply enamel mixture to the
40 mm × 40 mm polystyrene block.

craft shop. When you paint over the areas that you have left unscored, use a matt finish paint as the effect will be more realistic. Now mix two parts of grey enamel paint to one part of white enamel paint. To make your printing block, cut a piece of polystyrene tile into a 40 mm square. Rough the edges of the square with a knife and chip a few small pieces from the surface. This will give your final print a more textured effect. Paint the enamel mixture over the printing surface of the square before pressing down flat to print. It is a good idea to practise this on an old piece of paper, to make sure you are getting the right thickness of paint and right finger pressure.

Start printing over the previously applied paint, positioning your block square with the kitchen area corner. Each flagstone you print should be positioned about 1 mm from the one before. Keep the flagstones running in parallel lines across the floor area to be printed.

Ground floor interior walls

Dimensions for the ground floor walls are shown in the group of diagrams in figure 2.5. All of these should be made from 12 mm plywood except H. This is the corner fireplace in the morning room and should be made from 6 mm plywood. Details have been suggested in H and should be painted in. Details of the piece G can be found in figure 2.8. G comprises the wall for ground floor and upper floor alongside the staircase.

When all the walls have been cut out, slot piece B into the right of the hallway opening in piece A. Position these two pieces on the ground floor and check that they fall within the lines already marked out. Now do the same for all of the other pieces. As regards the door openings. F, G and D have their doors nearest to piece A. E and C have their doors furthest from piece A.

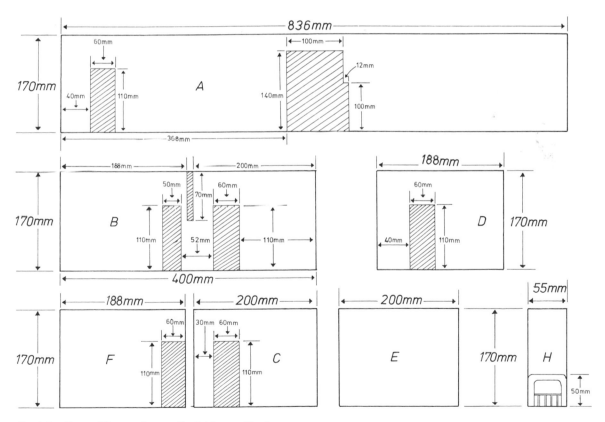

Fig. 2.5   Ground floor walls; see Fig. 2.4 for positioning.

To fix the walls to the floor, you will need to drill holes between the wall lines marked out on the ground floor. These holes must be positioned to miss door openings, and must be able to take no. 1 size 15 mm screws.

Before fixing the walls to the floor they should be painted and finished off with panelling and skirting boards cut from card. The skirting board is cut from 10 mm wide strips of white card and glued onto the walls at the floor edges. Run the strips around the door openings to represent the door frames. Panelling can be made from grey or white card, depending on the colour scheme of the rooms. The original rooms tend to be painted mid shades of eggshell blue, wedgewood blue, and gold and white.

Doors

At this stage you should make the doors. You will need five doors measuring 110 mm × 60 mm and one door measuring 110 mm × 50 mm. All should be cut from 6 mm plywood. Paint the doors white. When dry, paint on the panels with light grey paint. Brass door knobs can be represented by small upholstery nails or paper fasteners. To make the doors open, you will need to drive a 6 mm veneer pin into the lintel, 5 mm from the vertical edge of the door frame. Leave the veneer pin standing two or three mm proud of the wood, and cut off the head with pliers.

Having done this to all doorways, fit the walls to the floor again and mark a spot on the floor directly below each veneer pin. Remove the walls and drive veneer pins into the spots marked in the door openings on the floor. Cut off the heads of these pins, leaving them to protrude 2 or 3 mm from the wood. The cut-off will provide pivots on which the doors will hinge. Drill 1 mm holes, 5 mm in from an edge, at the top and bottom of each door. Slip the top of each door onto the pin in its lintel and check for clearance when swung open. When each door fits correctly, hold it in place with an elastic band. This will make it easier for you to slot the doors onto their floor pivots when fixing the walls in place. The elastic bands can be cut away once each wall has been glued and screwed to the floor. The walls C, D, E, F and G need to be fixed to wall A. Use veneer pins and glue. The heads of the pins can be touched up with paint once this has been done.

Hallway pillars

These are made from 140 mm long 15 mm diameter dowel, and should be positioned each side of the doorway between the hallway and the staircase area. Wrap plastic tape around one end of each dowel to represent the pillar bases. Paint these white. Now glue the pillars into position.

Now that the ground floor is complete it can be glued to the supports on the model base. The ends of

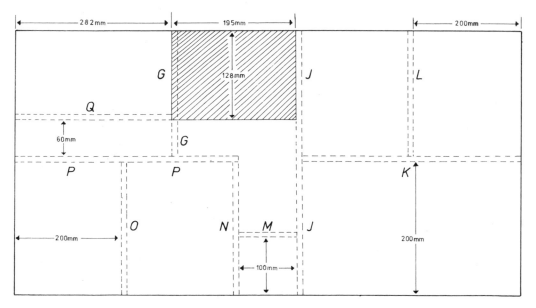

Fig. 2.6   Upper floor layout and base.

wall A should be veneer pinned to the side walls of the model. Now paint the inner surfaces of the side walls and add skirting and panels.

Upper floor

The upper floor is made from a sheet of 12 mm plywood. Using figure 2.6 as a guide, mark out the wall positions as you did on the ground floor. Cut away the shaded area. Now lay the upper floor sheet in place on the model with the staircase opening at the rear. Take a pencil and trace round the top of all the interior

Turn the upper floor sheet face upwards and score in the floorboard pattern, then varnish the entire top floor surface.

Figure 2.7 shows the wall pieces for the upper floor area. These are made from 12 mm plywood. Piece L in figure 2.6 is exactly the same as piece D in figure 2.5.

As regards the positioning of the walls. O has its doorway nearest P, which in turn has its doorway nearest the left-hand edge on the diagram. The doorway in Q is also nearest the left-hand edge of the diagram. J has its two doorways either side of K, with the narrower doorway nearest the staircase opening. G is

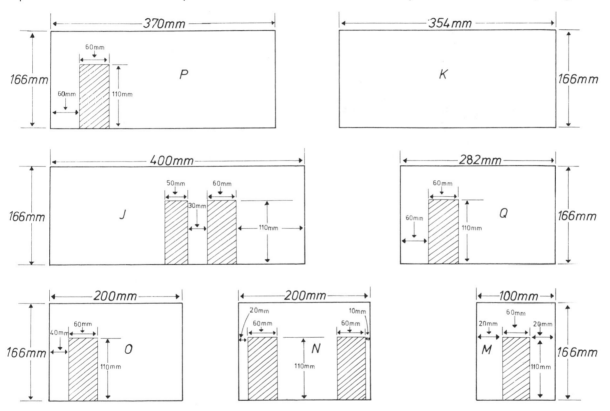

Fig. 2.7   Upper floor walls; see Fig. 2.5 for positioning.

walls on the ground floor, so that their pattern is transferred to the underside of the upper floor. Remove the upper floor sheet and lay it underside up on the bench. Now glue lengths of 18 mm concave quadrant beading around the lines, to provide cornicing for the ground floor rooms. Corners will have to be mitred for neatness, but any gaps can be filled with filler and sanded smooth. Having completed this, paint the cornicings and the ceilings white.

one piece and fits both floors, figure 2.8. Make and hang the doors, then paint and decorate the walls in the way that you did for the ground floor. Now fix the walls with glue and screw to the upper floor base. Fireplaces for the large drawing room and the sitting room beneath it can be made from blocks of wood and beading. Or you could buy Georgian-style dolls' house fireplaces to fit.

To fix the upper floor onto the model, coat the top edge of the ground floor walls with adhesive and slip the upper floor into place on the model. While the adhesive is still wet, apply pressure to the upper floor area. Using veneer pins, fix the side walls to the edges of K, P and Q. To finish this stage, add cornicing to the upper floor rooms.

Staircase

Turn the model around so that the back of the house faces you. On the left staircase opening you will see cracks where wall J and wall B join the upper floor. Fill these cracks and sand smooth before finishing off with a coat of paint.

Now cut two lower supports for the stairs. Use 12 mm plywood. Figure 2.9 shows the dimensions, with the stair positions indicated by broken lines. Glue one of the supports to the left wall of the staircase area, 6 mm in from back edge. Glue the second support so that it is parallel to the first support and its outer edge is 80 mm away from the left wall. Now cut out the two supports represented by figure 2.11. These are glued to the other side of the stair area. Cut the landing from 12 mm plywood. This is shown in figure 2.12. Plane or sand this to 10 mm thickness before gluing across the half-landing. The half-landing is the area half way up the stair supports.

You will need to cut sixteen steps from 10 mm thick wood fillet, see figure 2.10. Eight of these steps will fit across the lower supports and eight across the upper supports. The steps will probably need to be planed down to 9 mm thickness. Glue the steps in place across the supports. Now glue, 2.13, a piece of 6 mm

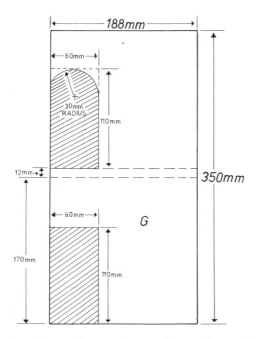

Fig. 2.8 Ground floor and upper floor wall, one piece, alongside staircase.

Fig. 2.9 (left)   Lower stairs support.

Fig. 2.10 (bottom left)   Step for staircase.

Fig. 2.11 (right)   Upper stairs support.

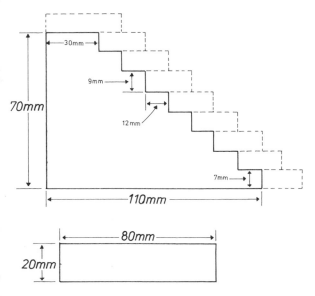

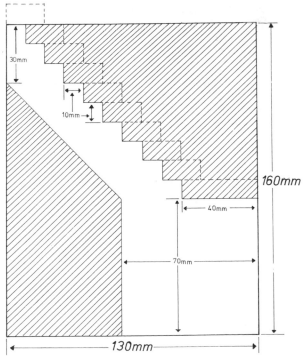

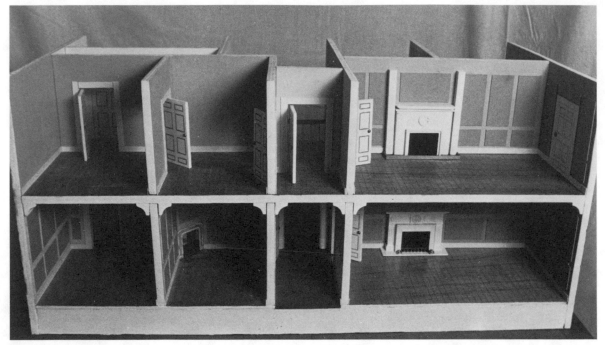

Front view of the completed interior.

Rear view of the model interior.

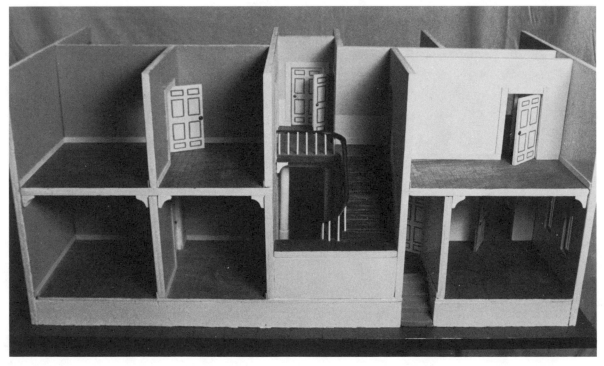

plywood across the back of the supports. This fits in below the half-landing and above the ground floor. Banisters can be made from matchsticks or from 2 mm diameter dowel which is obtainable from craft shops. The banisters should be 30 mm in length and the dowel should be fitted into holes drilled two to a step. It is a good idea to paint the banisters before fixing them in place. The top of the banisters should be made from a length of small diameter flexible tubing. Slit the tubing in half along its length, holding it length ways in a vice. Using impact adhesive glue it to the top of the rails. Stain or paint the stairs and handrail a mid golden-brown.

Fig. 2.12   Half-landing.

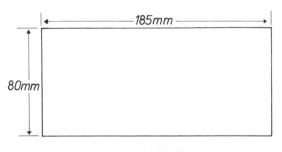

Fig. 2.13   Closure sheet for back of lower staircase support.

Front and rear walls

Figures 2.14 and 2.15 show the dimensions for the front and rear walls of the model. Make these from 12 mm plywood. The walls in the diagrams are laid out as they would fit onto the model. The narrow centre pieces in figures 2.14 and 2.15 are fixed to the model with veneer pins and adhesive. The other walls are hinged to the side walls of the model. But, before fixing these to the model you must finish off the windows and glaze them.

Windows

Check that all the window openings are reasonably square. Smooth them off with a file and glasspaper. Using 5 mm × 2 mm wood fillet or white card, glue window frames around the inside edge of the window openings. The frames should fit between the back and front face of the plywood walls. Once this is done paint the walls white on both sides, remembering that the side walls are painted white on the outside only. Most craftshops stock clear acetate and this should be used to make the windows. Cut the acetate sheet into pieces that will fit onto the back of the window frames. To give the glazing a window-pane effect paint white dividing lines onto the acetate sheet. The staircase window at the rear has eighteen window-panes. The window above the kitchen has eight panes. All the other windows have twelve panes. When the glazing sheets are made up, glue them in place behind their respective window frames.

Paint stone-coloured 10 mm wide frames around the windows to represent the architraves. The stone work trim, on the corners of the front of the house, should be painted on, and the flagstone pattern should be printed on the base around the model.

Fixing the outer walls

The narrow middle pieces in the centre of diagrams 2.14 and 2.15 should now be fixed in place at front and rear of the model. In each case use all three front or rear wallpieces to mark out the position of the fixed centre piece. The walls on either side of the fixed centre pieces are hinged to the side of the house. Use 10 mm wide 30 mm long brass hinges, two to a wall edge, to do this. For clearance while you fix the hinges, jack up each opening wall, 1 mm from the base, with a piece of card. The top edges of the hinged walls should be level with the other top edges of the model.

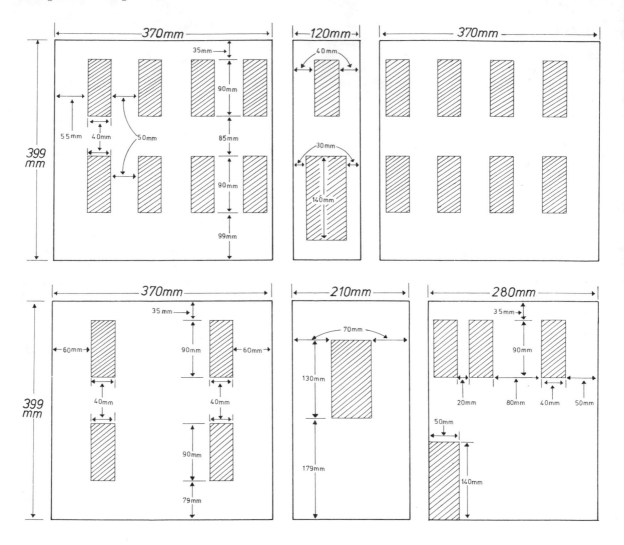

Fig. 2.14 (top)   Front walls as they will fit the model when it faces you.

Fig. 2.15   Rear walls as they will fit the model when the back of it faces you.

The rear of the model showing the hinged walls.

The roof

The roof base is made from 6 mm plywood measuring 880 mm × 420 mm, see figure 2.16. This diagram shows the positions of the gables, gable supports, roof supports and roof sheets. Select the side which will be upwards when the roof is on the building, shamfer its edges 5 mm at the front and sides. Using 12 mm plywood, cut three pieces of R, figure 2.17, for the gables, and three pieces of S, figure 2.18, for the gable supports. Figure 2.16 shows the positions of R and S when fixed together at the rear edge of the roof. Figure 2.19 shows the position of R and S on the base in cross-section. Fix these together with adhesive.

Next cut out three pieces of T, figure 2.20, for the roof supports. The positions of T are shown in figure 2.16. Cut roof sheet U, figure 2.21, from 6 mm plywood. Smooth with glasspaper and fix to the roof supports as shown in figure 2.16. This is the front face of the roof section. Note that the bottom edge of U must be level with the base edge. Now cut section V, figure 2.22, and fix this in place.

Having completed this stage you will now be ready to cut out the two side roof sheets W shown in figure 2.23. Fix the W sheets over the edges of U and V and the gables R. Note the roof sheets will overlap R. Still working with 6 mm plywood, check with figure 2.24, then cut four roof sheets X and glue these in place, see figure 2.16.

Now that the roof is assembled you will see gaps around the roof sheets. Fill these with a filler such as Plastic Padding. When dry, sand down the roof and paint it slate-grey. Tiles, or rather slates, can be scored onto the roof sides in the way that floorboard patterns were scored onto the floors of the interior. The capping tiles can be painted on the roof in a dull brick-red.

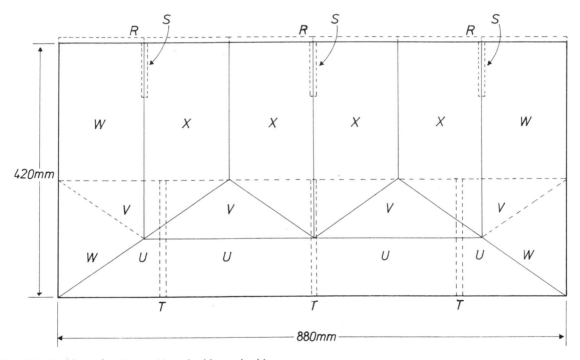

Fig. 2.16   Roof base showing position of gables and gable supports, and roof sheets and roof supports. Use the photograph of the back of the completed model to help you work out the positioning.

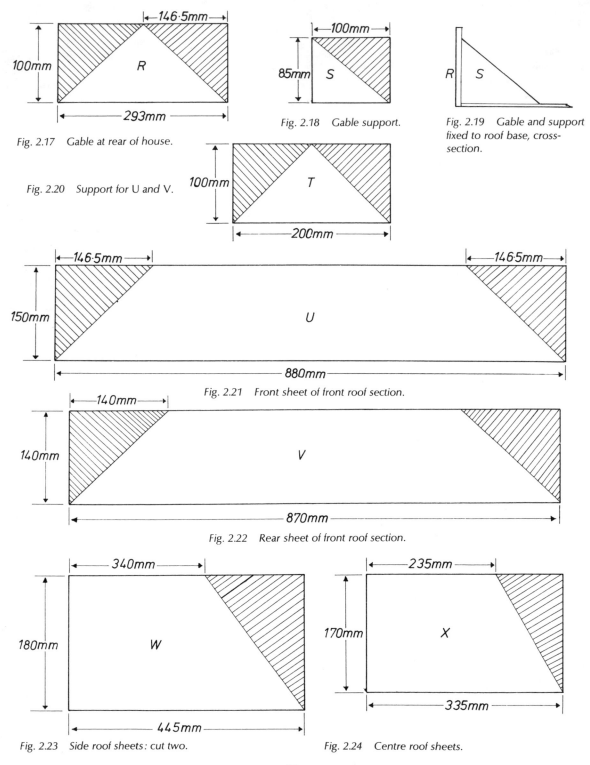

Fig. 2.17   Gable at rear of house.

Fig. 2.18   Gable support.

Fig. 2.19   Gable and support fixed to roof base, cross-section.

Fig. 2.20   Support for U and V.

Fig. 2.21   Front sheet of front roof section.

Fig. 2.22   Rear sheet of front roof section.

Fig. 2.23   Side roof sheets: cut two.

Fig. 2.24   Centre roof sheets.

Wordsworth House from the rear. The kitchen door fits into the right wall. Note the position of the chimneys.

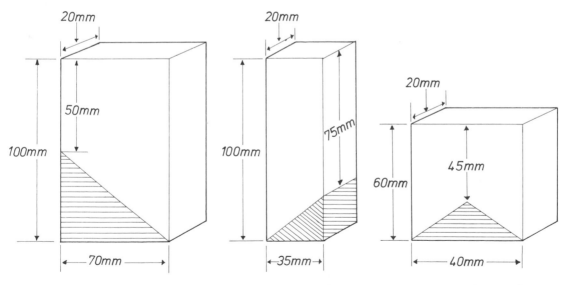

Fig. 2.25   Takes four chimney pots.   Fig. 2.26   Takes two chimney pots.   Fig. 2.27   Takes two chimney pots.

Chimneys

The main chimney-pieces can be made from blocks of wood or from strips of 20 mm × 10 mm fillet glued together to make the sizes given in figures 2.25, 2.26 and 2.27.

Figure 2.25 is the large chimney which appears on the right when the building is viewed from the back.

Figure 2.26 is the chimney to the left of the model. Figure 2.27 glues onto the top of the gable directly above the kitchen.

The chimneys should be decorated with a red brick pattern. You will find that 00 gauge brick embossed plastic sheet helps to achieve this effect. Cap the top of each chimney with a sheet of card slightly wider than the brick work. Paint this cap stone-grey. Use 20 mm lengths of tubing or dowel to make the chimney pots, which should be painted a dull brick-red. Fix the chimneys to the roof with Plastic Padding or similar epoxy resin glue.

Now that the roof is finished , it is a good idea to fix wooden stops a little in from the edges of its underside. These stops should be arranged to prevent the roof from slipping when in place.

Porch

Figures 2.28 and 2.30 show the side and front view of the porch. First make the base from 10 mm strips of wood. These strips of wood should be cut to the dimensions given in the diagrams, and then glued into a stack as shown. Next cut four pillar bases and four pillars. Glue the bases to the stack of wooden strips. Glue the pillars to the bases. The top of the porch is made from a 20 mm thick block of wood and is mounted onto the pillars with glue. The front and sides of the porch top are decorated with 10 mm wide beading. The broken lines on the diagrams show the position of the decoration. You will need to mitre the corners of the beading. To add further detail, cut a 20 mm wide strip out of the front edge of the beading strip, see figure 2.30. Glue the beading in place and then glue a piece of card across the 20 mm wide gap. Glue the 20 mm wide piece of beading on top of the card, this will give a raised effect to the centre head.

The steps for the porch are shown in figure 2.29 and are made from a stack of 10 mm thick wooden strips.

Cut and assemble as shown in the diagram. Sand the steps slightly to give them a worn appearance, then paint the porch and steps a mid stone-grey. Make the front door then glue the porch to the fixed centre wall. Glue the steps to the front of the porch. You should leave a 10 mm gap on either side of where the steps meet the porch.

Completed porch.

Fig. 2.28 (top left)   Side view of porch.

Fig. 2.29 (top centre)   Steps leading to porch.

Fig. 2.30 (top right)   Front view of porch. Notice how beading is cut at top of porch to make the 'centre head'.

Fig. 2.31 (bottom left)   Front door frame; broken lines show window-panes.

Fig. 2.32 (bottom centre)   One of the two front doors.

Fig. 2.33 (bottom right)   Rear door: cut as one piece. Broken lines show frame which should be painted on the glazing.

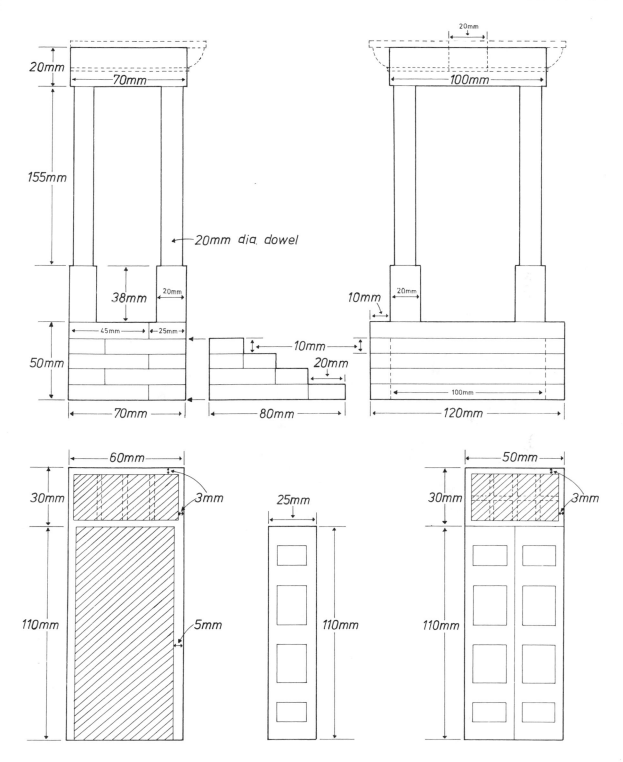

Outside doors

There are two doors to make for Wordsworth House. The one at the rear fixes to the opening right wall. The double door at the front is in the fixed centre wall.

Front Door

Refer to figure 2.31 and cut the door surround from thick white card. The top of this diagram shows the window-pane pattern. This should be drawn on clear acetate sheet. Cut a second identical door surround and glue on top of the first one, sandwiching the glazing portion. Cut two doors from the card, see figure 2.32. Score the panels onto each door and then paint brown. Using tape, hinge the doors to the door frame. A brass paper fastener will make a door handle. Now glue the edges of the door frame into the door opening at the front of the house.

Rear door

As with the front door, the rear door is a sandwich of two pieces of card around a piece of painted acetate sheet. Figure 2.33 shows the dimensions for this. Paint the door section brown leaving the top window frame white. When completed, glue into the door opening at the rear of the house so that the door becomes part of the opening wall section.

Rear steps

The rear passage steps, leading down to the rear door, are made from four 12 mm thick 50 mm wide strips of plywood. These are glued together in a stack, the edge of each step being 20 mm from the one before. The steps are painted stone-grey before being glued in place. Note the back of the stack must slip under the ground floor, while the edge of the first step lies level with the interior edge.

Completed model of Wordsworth House. The walls on either side of the fixed porch open to reveal the interior.

3   Fort William

A demand for beaver fur in the early nineteenth century, and the purchase of the Louisiana Territory from the French, started the westward movement of American fur trappers and traders. They travelled up the Missouri River and fanned out along its western tributaries, heading for the rich hunting grounds of the Rockies and the Great Plains. One of these tributaries was the River Platte, and the North Platte Route was travelled extensively for two decades before a fort was built in the region. It was called Fort William, after William Sublette one of the two fur traders who built it. The year was 1834, and the location the Laramie River some half a mile away from where it flowed into the North Platte. William Sublette and his companion Campbell were quick to see the potential of the area. It was rich in beaver, and the site was a natural meeting place for trappers, traders and indians. The fort gave protection against rival fur companies, unfriendly indians and the harsh winters, as well as serving the needs of travellers along what had become the great Oregon Trail. An artist named A J Miller visited the area in 1837 and the drawings and paintings he made of Fort William are the only surviving visual record of its appearance. Miller described the fort as 'a quadrangular form'. Block-houses were strategically placed at two diagonal corners to sweep the fronts with fire in time of attack. A larger blockhouse over the main entrance contained a cannon. At the rear of the fort was a secondary entrance, from which Miller made one of his paintings. Cabins were erected along three sides of the cottonwood palisade and contained a store room, blacksmith shop and living quarters. The fourth side of the fort was a corral for the horses. Indians visited the fort in large numbers and exchanged pelts for beads, tobacco, alcohol and dried food stuffs. Apparently they had a 'mortal horror' of the big gun or cannon. They had witnessed the destruction caused by its 'loud talk' and thinking that it was merely asleep, they dreaded its awakening.

Fort William changed ownership several times and in time also changed its name. This was said to be the work of a shipping clerk in St Louis. The clerk could not remember if some goods were intended for Fort William or for Fort John a nearby fort constructed in 1841. To complicate matters he knew there were other forts called Fort William in the Rocky Mountains. On asking what he should do he was told to mark all goods for Fort William, 'Fort William on the Laramie River'. Several days later, while marking goods, the clerk had a lapse of memory and marked them for 'Fort Laramie'. The name stuck and was used for all the forts built on that site after Fort William fell into decay.

The fur trade was declining and emphasis had moved to neighbouring Fort John. In 1849 the United States Government realised the need for an army post in the region and bought Fort Laramie. The rebuilding which followed turned Laramie into a military reservation resembling a small township.

The new Fort Laramie was to be instrumental in further historic events of the nineteenth century. The Indian tribes of the Great Plains, Sioux, Cheyenne and others, drew up important treaties at the fort in 1851 and 1868. It was a Pony Express station and a welcome stop for the Overland Stage. In 1876 it played an important part in the fight against Sitting Bull and the Sioux chiefs.

As ranching and homesteading grew, Fort Laramie once again became a place of protection for settlers. But its usefulness declined as order was brought to the area and in 1890 it was decided to abandon the fort. For 50 years Fort Laramie suffered the ravages of neglect and decay, but did not entirely disappear. Realising the sites national and historic importance the State of Wyoming made funds available for its purchase and subsequent donation to the United States Government.

From 1938 the Fort Laramie National Historic Site has been joined to the National Park system, who are taking great pains to restore it to its original structure.

The model that follows is based on paintings and descriptions made by A J Miller in 1837.

You will need

– the following tools

Drill with bits ranging from 1 mm to 2 mm drilling diameter plus a countersink bit.
Hammer.
Small hand saw.
Small craft saw or junior hacksaw.
Craft knife with spare blades.
Sawing block and mitre block.
Metric ruler, preferably steel.
Carpenter's square or set square.
Brushes.

– the following materials

One piece of 12 mm plywood or chipboard, 600 mm × 550 mm, for base of model.
Two pieces of 5 mm plywood, 500 × 100 mm, for front and rear walls.
Two pieces of 5 mm plywood, 400 mm × 100 mm, for side walls.
Eight pieces of 5 mm plywood, 80 mm × 60 mm, for cabin supports.
Three pieces of 5 mm plywood, 80 mm × 50 mm, for side cabin supports.
One piece of 5 mm plywood, 150 mm × 60 mm, for cabin walls.
One piece of 5 mm plywood, 198 mm × 60 mm, for cabin walls.
One piece of 5 mm plywood, 265 mm × 60 mm, for cabin walls.
One piece of 5 mm plywood, 160 mm × 60 mm, for cabin walls.
One piece of 5 mm plywood, 155 mm × 60 mm, for cabin walls.
One piece of 3 mm plywood, 150 mm × 60 mm, for cabin roofs.
One piece of 3 mm plywood, 198 mm × 60 mm, for cabin roofs.
One piece of 3 mm plywood, 325 mm × 50 mm, for cabin roofs.
One piece of 3 mm plywood, 430 mm × 60 mm, for cabin roofs.
Eight pieces of 3 mm plywood, 85 mm × 50 mm, for corner blockhouse roofs.
Two pieces of 3 mm plywood, 90 mm × 65 mm, for main blockhouse roof.

Two pieces of 3 mm plywood, 130 mm × 48 mm, for main blockhouse roof.
Two pieces of 5 mm plywood, 103 mm × 70 mm, for main entrance enclosure.
One piece of 5 mm plywood, 103 mm × 100 mm, for main entrance enclosure.
One piece of 5 mm plywood, 135 mm × 110 mm, for main blockhouse floor.
Two pieces of 3 mm plywood, 110 mm × 70 mm, for main blockhouse sides.
Two pieces of 3 mm plywood, 80 mm × 75 mm, for main blockhouse sides.
1120 mm of 5 mm plywood strip, 20 mm wide, for palisade walkways.
320 mm of 5 mm plywood strip, 25 mm wide, for palisade walkway, corral.
Two pieces of 3 mm plywood, 75 mm × 75 mm, for corner blockhouse floors.
Four pieces of 3 mm plywood, 75 mm × 65 mm, for corner blockhouse sides.
Three pieces of 3 mm plywood, 83 mm × 65 mm, for corner blockhouse side.
One piece of 3 mm plywood, 103 mm × 83 mm, for rear corner blockhouse side.
One piece of 3 mm plywood, 50 mm × 30 mm, for walking stage.
500 mm of hardwood strip, 10 mm × 3 mm, for ladders.
3 m of hardwood strip, 5 mm × 3 mm, for palisade capping, rails and fence.
600 mm of hardwood strip, 5 mm × 5 mm, for rail and fence posts.
700 mm of wood fillet, 10 mm × 10 mm, for palisade walkway supports.
100 mm of 6 mm diameter tube, plastic or metal, for cabin chimneys.
About 2 kilos of dry fine sand for ground of fort.
3 m of wood fillet or beading, 20 mm × 10 mm, for base surround.
Various offcuts of wood fillet or beading, 20 mm × 10 mm, for palisade supports to base inside cabins.
25 mm veneer pins and 10 mm fine veneer pins.
Three matchsticks or similar.
Wood adhesive.
Contact adhesive.
Small tin modeller's paint, slate-grey and black.
Glasspaper.
Tube of epoxy resin or similar.

To begin your model

Mark out the base

As long as the baseboard for this model is sound and flat, it need not be in prime condition as any surface scratches will be covered up with sand. Make sure your board is at least 12 mm thick and 600 mm × 550 mm. Refer to figure 3.1 and mark out the baseboard as shown. Edge the base with 20 mm × 10 mm wood fillet. You can either mitre or butt joint the corners. When you have finished this, turn the board so that it is positioned as in figure 3.1. The edge facing you must be the front of the fort. The rear of the fort will correspond to the top of the diagram.

the front and rear. The cut away corners on A and B are to take the corner blockhouses when the walls are erected.

Having completed this stage and sanded the edges, each wall piece should be scored, front and back, to give a log or planking effect. Use the scoring technique described in Chapter 2. Score each line 10 mm apart and run a pencil down each line for extra effect. Remember that the gates will need to be scored in the same way. There are two gates to each entrance, each gate opening at the centre. So you will need to cut your gate pieces into two identical halves. For information on how to fit these gates see the section marked *Doors* in Chapter 2.

Having drilled the doors and fixed them temporarily

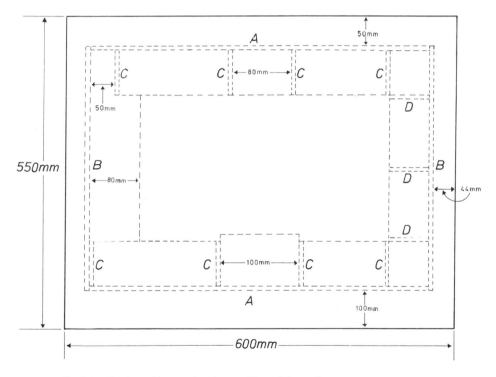

Fig. 3.1   Baseboard layout showing position of the walls.

Palisade

The palisade is made from 5 mm thick plywood which should be cut out with a craft knife. Figures 3.2 and 3.3 show the dimensions for the walls. Cut two of each. When cutting the palisade walls A try to remove the entrance pieces so that they can be reused as gates at

into place with elastic bands, the palisade pieces should be mounted on the baseboard. Use contact adhesive, and veneer pins hammered through the baseboard into the bottom edge of each wall. First mount the A pieces onto the baseboard, making sure blockhouse openings go to the front right and rear left of the model. Now fix the B pieces to the baseboard making sure that the blockhouse openings correspond. When the walls are set firm, check the gates are opening properly and then cap the top of the palisade with 5 mm wide wood strip. Make knife cuts across the capping, every 100 mm or so, to obtain a plank effect. The walls should now be strengthened with 20 mm × 10 mm battens or beading. Fix the

battens between the lines marked for C and D. C and D are the cabin wall supports. One edge of the batten should be glued to the inside of the palisade and the other edge to the base. When the cabin walls are fixed in place, the battens will be hidden. Note that in the photograph of the baseplan, C and D have been cut to fit over the beading, rather than the beading being cut to fit between C and D.

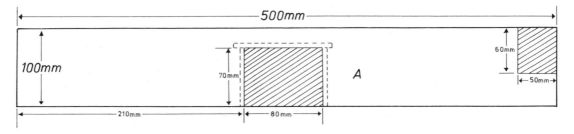

Fig. 3.2 Front and back palisade wall: cut two.

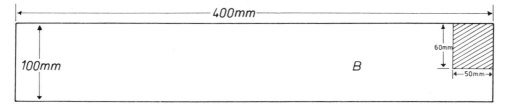

Fig. 3.3   Side palisade wall: cut two.

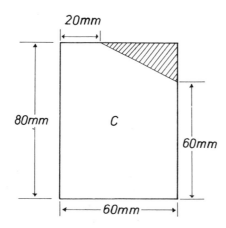

Fig. 3.4   Front and back cabin wall support: cut eight.

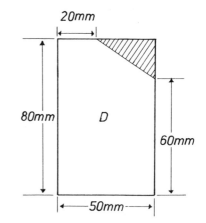

Fig. 3.5   Side cabin wall support: cut three.

Palisade and cabin walls on a chipboard base. The spaces at the two corners are for the corner blockhouses.

Cabin wall supports

Refer to figures 3.4 and 3.5 and cut eight pieces of *C* and three pieces of *D* from 5 mm plywood. These should be glued in place on the base against the palisade. One side of each rear support *C* faces into the rear entrance enclosure and should be scored to give a plank effect. The two front supports *C* which fix to the sides of the front entrance enclosure, should not be glued into place at this stage.

Front Entrance Enclosure

Using bottom half of figure 3.15, cut three entrance enclosure pieces from 5 mm plywood. Score the face of each piece. Take doorway entrance piece and lay it flat against inside of palisade, so it matches up with front entrance. Run a pencil around the edges where they touch palisade. Remove the doorway piece and glue the side enclosure pieces within these lines. Check for squareness, then glue the doorway to the side enclosure pieces. Glue the two remaining cabin wall supports to side walls of entrance enclosure.

Cabin walls

The cabin walls are made from 5 mm plywood. Figures 3.6 to 3.10 show the dimensions for these. The doors and windows are the same size in each piece, the windows being cut out, the doors being scored into the wood with a knife. Scoring a 5 mm surround around each door will add realism as will the use of vertical scored planking effect on the door surface. The scoring lines on the rest of the cabin wall surfaces should run horizontally, with a 10 mm gap between each line. Score in log ends at each end of the wall. A line of log ends should be placed midway on the wall in figure 3.8. Log ends signify where an inner wall of logs would have been built to divide the cabin interiors into rooms. There are no records of the room sizes of the cabins, but we can imagine the rough location of the rooms.

Glue the cabin walls to the edges of the cabin wall supports and the base. When looked at from the back of the fort, the wall, in figure 3.6, is glued to the left of the main entrance, with its door nearest the side enclosure wall. The wall in figure 3.7 is glued to the right of the main entrance. Next, looking at the model from the front, glue the long wall, figure 3.8, to the

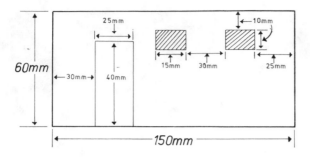

Fig. 3.6 Cabin wall to left of main blockhouse. (Looking from inside of quadrangle.)

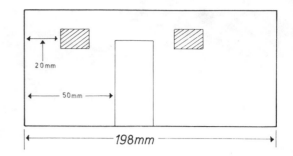

Fig.3.7 Cabin wall to right of main blockhouse. (Looking from inside of quadrangle.)

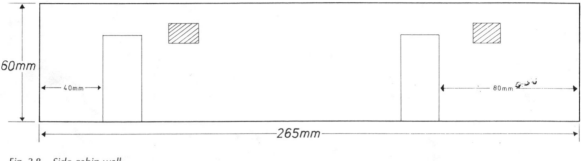

Fig. 3.8 Side cabin wall.

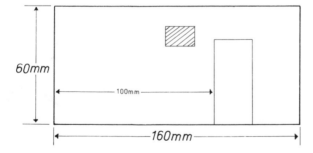

Fig. 3.9 Rear cabin wall between rear entrance and corner blockhouse.

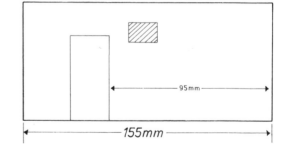

Fig. 3.10 Right side, rear cabin wall.

supports D on the right side of the model. The walls in figures 3.9 and 3.10 are glued in place, left and right, to the rear cabin wall supports.

Palisade walkway

The walkway, or firing stage, around the inner side of the palisade is made from strips of 5 mm plywood. The cabin wall supports carry this around the front, rear and right side of the fort. Each strip of walkway should be 20 mm wide. You will need two walkways for the front cabins, one either side of the entrance. One walkway to run down the right side cabins. And one walkway to run across the rear cabins. Four in all. The rear walkway should cover the rear entrance enclosure and stop at the support of the rear left cabin. This will allow space for the rear corner blockhouse. The walkway above the corral is added later.

Cabin roofs

Using 3 mm plywood, cut two roofs to fit across the

60

front cabins. These should be 60 mm deep. Looked at from the front the roof on the left cabin runs from the palisade wall to the side of the entrance enclosure. The roof of the right cabin runs from the right side of the entrance enclosure to C, the right cabin support nearest the front right corner. Before fixing the right-hand roof, cut a square of wood, 15 mm × 15 mm, from the lower right-hand corner of the roof. Glue the two front cabin roofs in place. Now refer to figure 3.11 and cut out the side cabin roof. Glue this in place so that it slots against the roof of the right front cabin. The remaining roof, figure 3.12, fits across the two rear cabins and the rear entrance enclosure.

Ground texture

Before adding further detail to the model, it is a good idea to texture the ground inside the fort. You will need a kilo of thoroughly dried coarse sand, not too red in colour. Using a fairly fluid wood glue, paint the surface of the base inside the fort. Do not forget the inside of the entrance enclosures. Sprinkle the sand over the glued surface while the glue is still wet. Be fairly liberal with the amount of sand you use and use a spoon to help sprinkle the sand into the corners. Let the model dry for a day or so and then brush off the surplus sand. To add further realism score cart tracks on the sand while it is drying.

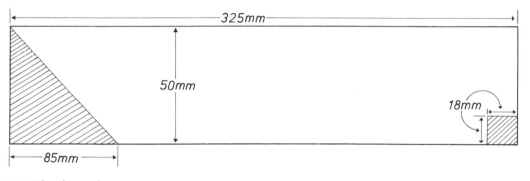

Fig. 3.11   Side cabin roof.

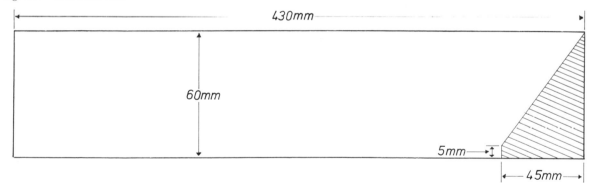

Fig. 3.12   Rear cabin roof.

As the roofs were probably tiled you can either use tile paper or else score tiles onto the roofs before fixing the roofs in place. Chimneys can be made from 5 mm diameter tubing, painted black to resemble stove pipes. Make each chimney 20 mm long and cut the bottom at an angle to suit the roof. If you have scored the roofs, you will need to paint them slate-grey. Do this before fixing the chimneys in place.

Blockhouse roofs

The shapes for the main blockhouse roof, are shown in figure 3.13. Cut two of each size from 3 mm plywood. To assemble, coat the sloping edges with contact adhesive. When the adhesive is nearly dry arrange the pieces so that the two smaller ones are opposite each other. All four pieces should have their points touching. Press the edges together, so that you form a roof that meets at a central point. Fill any gaps along the joins with epoxy resin. When the top side is dry, turn over the roof and do the same to the joins on the under side. When under side has set hard, turn the roof the right way up and glasspaper the top edges.

To finish off the roof, drill a hole at the central point. This is to take a matchstick. Smooth the matchstick to a tapered point and glue into the hole. Paint the roof slate-grey. The roof can later be glued to the blockhouse walls, or it can be left to lift off.

The two roofs for the corner blockhouses are similar in construction to the main blockhouse roof. Figure 3.14 shows the dimensions for the four sections which make up each roof.

lengths of 10 mm × 10 mm wood fillet. Figure 3.15 shows the dimensions for the log support. Set the support 30 mm from the palisade wall. Refer to figure 3.16 and cut out the blockhouse floor, this should be 110 mm × 135 mm. Score a planking effect onto both sides of the floor. Now glue the floor in place on the top edges of the entrance enclosure. The floor should overlap the entrance enclosure by 5 mm all round.

The walls of the blockhouse are cut from 3 mm plywood, see figure 3.16. Cut these pieces and score them with a planking effect. Cut out the firing slits, in rows of three. The firing slits measure 10 mm × 10 mm. Now cut the larger firing holes and the doorway. Assemble the walls with contact adhesive, fixing the front and rear walls first.

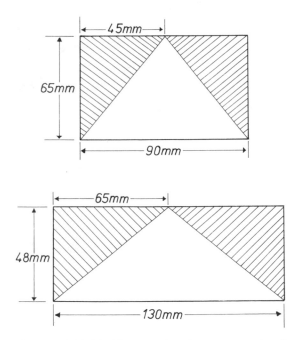

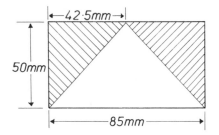

Fig. 3.14   Corner blockhouse roof section: cut eight.

Fig. 3.13   Main blockhouse roof sections: cut two of each.

Corner blockhouses

The corner blockhouses are of a similar construction to the main blockhouse. Figure 3.17 shows the dimensions for the front corner blockhouse. Make this from 3 mm plywood with a 75 mm × 75 mm floor. Scoring is the same as for the main blockhouse. The two firing slits are 10 mm × 10 mm set centrally on the sides, 20 mm down from the top edge. While the completed blockhouse is setting, glue a 40 mm block of wood in the square formed by supports C and D, see figure 3.1. This is to support the blockhouse floor. Now glue the blockhouse into the front corner, so that its two firing slits face outwards from the palisade.

The rear corner blockhouse is slightly different from the front corner one. The side marked X in figure 3.17 is replaced by the side shown in figure 3.18. This will allow the inner-facing walls to slot between the end of the cabins, the corral and the corner of the palisade.

Main blockhouse

The main blockhouse is mounted on top of the front entrance enclosure. Its floor is made from 5 mm plywood supported outside the palisade by three

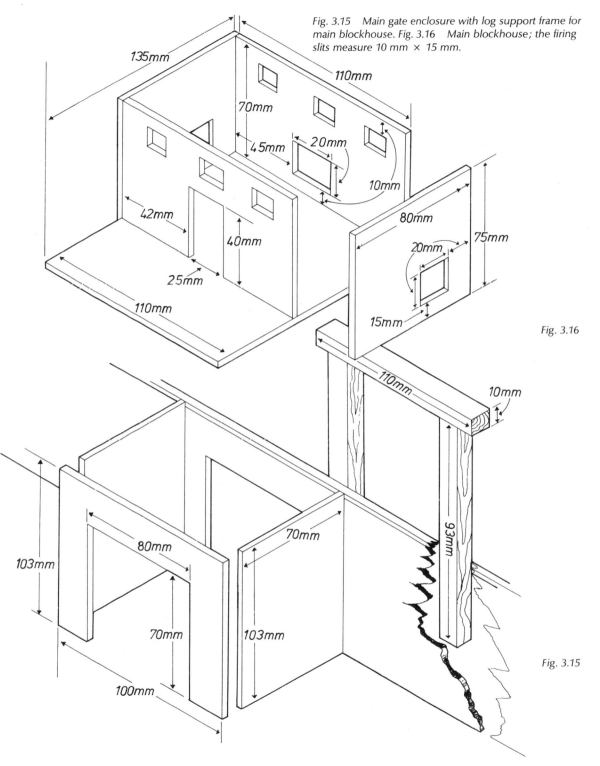

Fig. 3.15   Main gate enclosure with log support frame for main blockhouse. Fig. 3.16   Main blockhouse; the firing slits measure 10 mm × 15 mm.

135mm

110mm

70mm

45mm

20mm

10mm

42mm

40mm

25mm

110mm

80mm

75mm

20mm

15mm

Fig. 3.16

110mm

10mm

70mm

93mm

80mm

103mm

70mm

103mm

70mm

100mm

Fig. 3.15

Inner view of the fort showing the main blockhouse with its ladders, rails and walkway. Note the gate in the corral fencing to the right of the photograph.

Corral walkway

The corral walkway is supported on four of the beam and pole structures shown in figure 3.19. These are joined to the palisade and base. Each one is made from 10 mm × 10 mm fillet. Fix one next to the rear blockhouse, one next to the front left cabin. The other two are fixed at equal intervals between the first two. You will need to cut away a square of the surface texture to allow each support pole to sit square and firm on the base.

Take a strip of 5 mm plywood 25 mm wide. This is the walkway and should run from the front cabin roof to the rear corner blockhouse. Shamfer one end to fit snugly on top of the cabin roof. Glue the walkway in place.

Slotting the rear corner blockhouse into place.

Corral fence

The corral fence is made from 5 mm × 5 mm wood strip and 10 mm × 3 mm wood strip. Cut seven

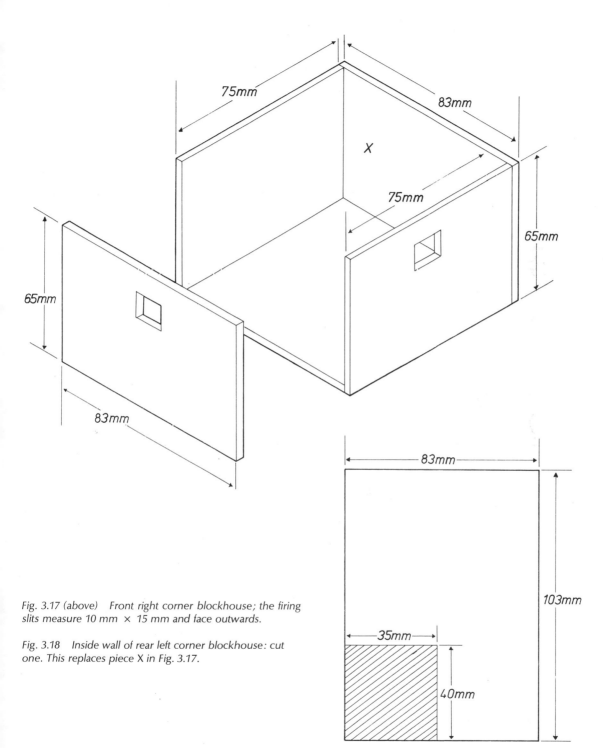

Fig. 3.17 (above)   Front right corner blockhouse; the firing slits measure 10 mm × 15 mm and face outwards.

Fig. 3.18   Inside wall of rear left corner blockhouse: cut one. This replaces piece X in Fig. 3.17.

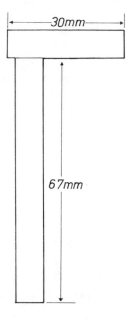

Fig. 3.19   *Support for the corral walkway: make four.*

40 mm long fence posts from the 5 mm × 5 mm strip. Two lengths of 10 mm × 3 mm strip are then glued horizontally across the fence posts. You will need one length 80 mm long, another 140 mm long, and a smaller 35 mm strip to serve as a gate. Glue the fence posts to the base, 80 mm from the palisade wall, refer to figure 3.1. The shorter fence is set at the end of the corral nearest the main blockhouse. The gate can be hinged or else glued in place. Make two handrail sections for the inner rear entrance enclosure. These should fit between the cabin fronts. Leave a gap between the handrails.

Main blockhouse handrail

The main blockhouse handrail is situated on the upper floor section, looking into the fort. Posts are made from 30 mm lengths of 5 mm × 5 mm wood strips. These should be glued around the exposed edges of the upper floor. Looking from the back of the fort, leave a gap in the left-hand rails to take the steps from the cabin roof. To make the rails, add a 5 mm wide strip to the top of the posts, mitring the corners if possible.

Steps to main blockhouse and walkway

Refer to figure 3.21 and cut two strips, 3 mm thick. Mark off eight step positions, 10 mm apart. The steps are cut from 3 mm strip to the size shown in figure 3.22. Using contact adhesive, fix the eight steps to one of the side strips. Rest this strip on a table top with the step ends facing upward. Glue the other strip in place and check for squareness, before fixing the steps to the base and cabin, 30 mm from the entrance enclosure wall.

Cut the walking stage shown in figure 3.20. Use 3 mm plywood. Shamfer the underside of the end which will meet the roof. Check that the walking stage will fit between the ladder sides and will run level with the point where the cabin roof meets the palisade walkway. Glue in place.

The upper steps are similar in construction to the lower steps. Figure 3.23 shows the side strips. Glue the steps shown in figure 3.22 to a side strip. Glue the other side strip in place. Now glue the steps from the small walking stage to the edge of the main blockhouse floor. The top of the steps should fit into the gaps left in the handrail.

To finish the fort, add sand texture to the surrounding base of the model and paint the edge of the base. Model figures of frontiersmen and indians fit the fort, while the addition of small cannons and horses can make the whole fort come alive.

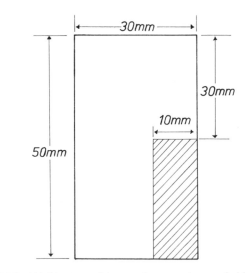

Fig. 3.20   *Walking stage between lower and upper ladders to main blockhouse.*

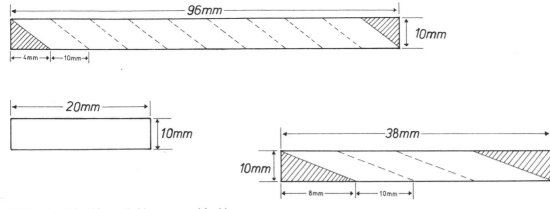

Fig. 3.21 (top)   Side of lower ladder to main blockhouse:
cut two.

Fig. 3.22 (middle)   Lower and upper ladder steps: cut ten.

Fig. 3.23 (bottom right)   Side of upper ladder to main
blockhouse: cut two.

The completed model of Fort William.

4 Harlech Castle

The remains of Harlech Castle on the northern coastal curve of Cardigan Bay are a dramatic reminder of the turbulence of Welsh history. Although simple in design, in its time it was a pinnacle of Edwardian fortification.

The castle was built by James of St George who was in charge of designing Edward I's new fortifications in Wales. It was built between 1285 and 1290 and James of St George was constable of the castle until 1293.

When the construction work was at its height, there were 227 masons, 22 carpenters, 115 quarrymen, 30 smiths, and 546 labourers employed on the site. Limestone was brought by ship from Anglesey and Caernarvon, while Chester provided iron and steel. On completion the total cost was between £9,500 and £10,000, a fortune at the time.

The castle dominated the coast line. Its main form of defence was a massive gatehouse which faced inland. A moat bounded the castle to the south and the east. The inner ward contained the domestic buildings and had large towers at all four corners. A wall walk connected the towers. The gatehouse also had towers. Two of these looked inward and were there in case they were needed to overawe a mutinous garrison. The gatehouse was also designed as a constable's residence. The wall surrounding the inner ward was protected by an outer ward and by ramparts. This provided the castle with two levels from which bowmen could simultaneously unleash a hail of arrows.

The English held Harlech Castle until 1404, when it was captured by Owain Glyndwr. Harlech was Glyndwr's capital for four years and it is believed that he held a parliament within the castle walls. Although Charles VI of France sent men to help Glyndwr, Harlech fell to the English in 1408.

Harlech was to figure again in the Wars of the Roses. Dafydd ap Ieuan sided with the Lancastrians and held the castle while Queen Margaret took refuge there.

The Lancastrians were defeated, but Harlech held out until the end and was the last castle to fall. The song 'March of the Men of Harlech' commemorates this event.

By the reign of Elizabeth 1, the former glory of Harlech was at an end. Only the gatehouse was habitable and this was utilised as a judge's lodgings during the Assize.

During the Civil Wars, the crumbling walls of Harlech were beseiged by Roundhead troops, who eventually forced Colonel William Owen to surrender.

The castle has been in the care of the state since 1914, and the post of constable still survives, although the gatehouse is no longer used as his residence.

In making my model of Harlech Castle I used polystyrene and plaster of paris as my main materials. These are fairly inexpensive and are easy to use.

Polystyrene can be bought in sheet form and the sheets glued together to build up the required dimensions. However, the model featured here was made from the discarded polystyrene packaging of a shower unit. So cast around for unwanted pieces before buying.

Plaster of paris is obtainable from chemists and is often labelled 'dental plaster'. It hardens quickly when poured into a mould so it is advisable to practise using plaster of paris before starting the model.

You will need

– the following tools

Hand saw.
Mitre block (optional).
Hammer.
Small razor saw or a junior hacksaw, obtainable from craft shops.
Craft knife with supply of long blades.
Large knife.
Scissors.
Metric ruler, preferably steel.
Square or set square.
Compasses.
Fibre tipped pen for marking polystyrene.
Painting brushes.
Plastic bowl or carton for mixing plaster of paris.

– the following materials

One sheet of carbon-paper, 600 mm × 550 mm.
One sheet of tracing-paper, 600 mm × 550 mm.
One polystyrene slab, 600 mm × 500 mm × 120 mm, for main castle foundation, or four sheets of polystyrene, 600 mm × 500 mm × 30 mm.
About two thirds of the above quantity again of polystyrene to make curtain walls, inner buildings etc.

One piece of plywood, 600 mm × 550 mm × 6 mm, for base of model.
Two pieces of woodstrip, 600 mm × 20 mm × 10 mm, for model base edging.
Two pieces of woodstrip, 550 mm × 20 mm × 10 mm, for model base edging.
One piece of thick card, 600 mm × 500 mm, for templates and roofs.
One piece of balsawood, 265 mm × 90 mm × 10 mm, for back corner of outer ward.
About 9 kilos of plaster of paris, buy 3 kilos at a time.
One 1 kilo pack of self-hardening model clay, from a craft shop.
Two or three wood offcuts to make barbican gate and bridge.
Adhesive suitable for gluing polystyrene to wood.
One small tube of Araldite or similar resin glue.
One pack of filler, the type available for use on all materials, from a decorating shop.
Small quantity of dry sand.
Various grades of glasspaper.
Veneer pins.
Poster paints; do not use oil or cellulose based paints on polystyrene.
Several large Fairy Liquid bottles or similar, for the moulds.
Roll of clear sticky tape.
Large wad of Plasticine or similar.
Paper clips.

To begin your model

Mark out the model base

Take a piece of plywood 600 mm × 550 mm × 6 mm and strengthen the underside of each edge with 20 mm × 10 mm woodstrip. The corners of the stripping may either be mitred or butt jointed. The edging strip should be glued and veneer pinned to the plywood.

To mark out the baseboard, obtain a piece of tracing-paper 600 mm × 550 mm. Examine figure 4.1, then rule the paper into 50 mm squares. Using the squares as a guide, copy the castle plan onto the paper. You can use compasses and a ruler to do this. Now put the tracing-paper on the baseboard so it registers square with the edges. Tape two corners of the tracing-paper to the base and push a piece of carbon-paper between the tracing-paper and the plywood. Using a pencil, trace the line bordering sections A and A–B in figure 4.1. This outer line will be used to position the polystyrene foundation.

Now trace the entire castle plan onto a piece of thick card, 600 mm × 550 mm. Take the card and cut round the line containing sections A and A–B. This is your template for marking out the polystyrene sheets and its shape should be the same as the shape drawn on the baseboard.

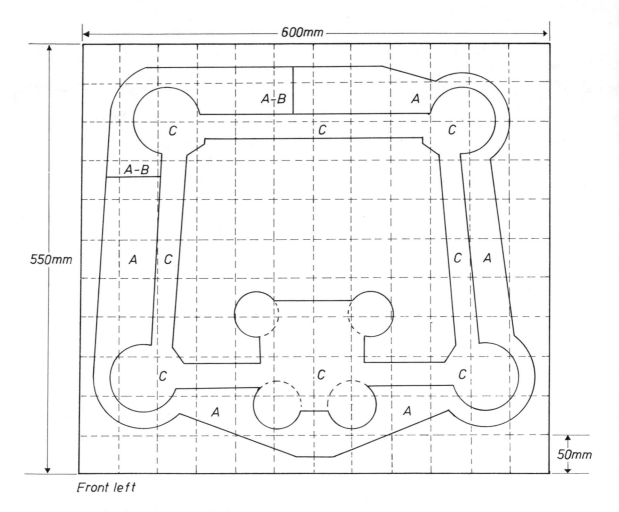

Fig. 4.1   Baseboard and template layout; broken lines are pencil construction lines on tracing-paper.

Foundations

The castle foundations include the outer ward ramparts. Look at figure 4.2 which shows a cross-section of the foundations. You can cut the foundations from a solid slab of polystyrene or from four 30 mm sheets or use eight 15 mm thick sheets. But remember, whatever its thickness, each sheet of polystyrene should measure 600 mm × 550 mm.

To mark out the polystyrene sheets, rest the template in position and draw around the edge with a fibre tipped pen. When all the sheets have been marked out, cut away the outer waste with a craft knife.

Take the baseboard and coat the foundation area with a polystyrene/wood glue. Put the first sheet of polystyrene in place and weight it down until the adhesive is dry. If this first sheet of polystyrene is less than 30 mm thick, add a further sheet as you will need to bring the thickness up to 30 mm.

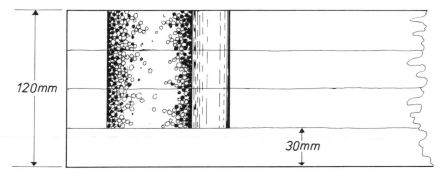

Fig. 4.2   Side view of left-hand rear corner, showing how polystyrene slabs are stuck together with cut-away for A-B section.

The castle foundations are made from polystyrene layers glued with PVA adhesive. The edges of the polystyrene have been given a rough coat of plaster.

Now take the template and cut away the section marked A–B, this area surrounds the rear left tower, see figure 4.1. Using this new template, cut out the remaining sheets of polystyrene. Glue these on top of the first sheet already stuck to the baseboard. Figure 4.2 shows a side view of the rear left corner. Do not destroy the template as you will need it again.

Ramparts and wall, rear left corner

The rear left corner of the model should now have two steps, each one stepping down to the area surrounding the base of the tower. By using pieces of polystyrene and plaster of paris, slope the steps to form a dip at the corner. When you turn the step into a dip, leave a 10 mm gap around the edge of the foundations, so the walls can be fitted into place.

Refer to figures 4.3 and 4.4 and cut the two walls from balsawood. Using an all purpose ready-mixed filler, fix the wall pieces in place. The walls curve around the tower and are fixed against the sloping work you have just completed. Figure 4.3 is the rear corner wall and figure 4.4 the side corner wall.

You should be left with a gap between the walls. This gap needs a curved wall built into it. To do this, cut two curved pieces from a plastic washing-up-liquid bottle. Tape one piece to the inner edge and one piece to the outer edge of the balsawood walls. The outer piece will need to reach down to the model base. Press Plasticine around the bottom edges of the plastic curves. You now have a mould prepared for your curved wall piece. The wall should be 10 mm thick. Mix up a small quantity of fairly liquid plaster of paris. Pour this into the mould until it is 2 mm deep. Allow this to set for fifteen minutes before mixing more plaster and filling the mould level with the adjoining balsawood walls. Allow the casting to set hard before removing the plastic.

Casting the wall at the rear left corner. The ramparts to the right and left are made from balsawood.

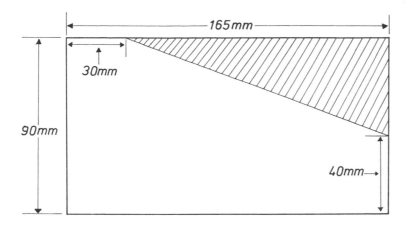

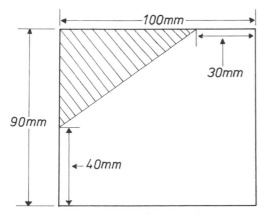

Fig. 4.3 (above)   Rear wall, 10 mm thick, cut for rear left corner.

Fig. 4.4 (left)   Side wall, cut for rear left corner.

Moat walls and bridge

As was explained in the introduction, the castle had a moat around its south and its east side, that is, the left side and the front of the model. This moat was crossed by a bridge from the barbican gate to the hinterland. There was a moat retaining wall at the Weathercock Tower corner, rear left, with another moat retaining wall at the north east corner, front right. For the purposes of this model, only a small section of the bridge is used. This should be made from wood strip 100 mm × 20 mm × 10 mm, glued in place below the barbican gate position, with a gap at the top for steps to be added.

Only the rear left moat retaining wall needs to be added to the model. This should be made from balsawood, 60 mm × 40 mm × 10 mm, and should be glued in place 50 mm from the rear left corner, angled back towards the rear left corner of the baseboard.

Finishing off the outer ward ramparts

Whether you made the foundations from one single slab, or from several sheets of polystyrene, the edges will be rough and pitted. To smooth these, mix a quantity of plaster of paris and apply a thin layer of plaster all around the outer ward in the same way as you would ice a cake. Use a spatula or stiff piece of card. Make sure you cover the joins between the two balsawood walls and the polystyrene. When the plaster is dry, smooth off with fine glasspaper. Any pits remaining in the surface can be filled in with more plaster.

Landscaping

Use polystyrene to represent rocks and soil around the base of the model. Use the template to cut 30 mm thick pieces of polystyrene to fit around the curved corners. As a guide, the landscaping is higher on the right side of the model, than on the left. Do not build up to more than three 30 mm thicknesses at any one point. The edges of the polystyrene should be broken to add texture. Any large gaps in the polystyrene can be filled in with plaster.

Marking out the towers and inner ward

Take the template and cut away the inner ward area, see figure 4.1. Using a fibre tipped pen mark an outline of the inner ward area onto the model. Now cut away section A of the template. Your template should now comprise the plan of the towers, the curtain wall and the gatehouse. Position the template on top of the foundations and draw around the template. You should now have transferred area C to the polystyrene.

Cutting out the outer ward ramparts

Area A, the outer ward, should now have a border drawn 10 mm in from its outer edge. This is the thickness of the ramparts. With a sharp knife, cut along this border line, and along the outline of the towers, gatehouse front, and curtain wall. Now dig out the area between these two lines. Dig to a depth of 15 mm. Do not do this around the rear left corner. The 10 mm thick ramparts should run flush into the balsawood walls.

Making the towers

The towers at the corners and around the gatehouse are cast from plaster of paris. To make moulds for the corner towers, use two large plastic washing-up-liquid bottles per tower. Cut the tops and bottoms off the bottles. Now cut lengthways along each cylinder so that it will open out. The moulds should be 180 mm high.

Carefully fit one opened out bottle around the curve of each semi circular shape already cut into the foundations. You will need to cut away sections of the moulds where the mould crosses the curtain wall C.

Casting the main corner towers. The outer ward has been dug out with a knife. The mould at the centre of the picture has just been removed from the front right tower. The rear towers are still setting.

Fit a second precut plastic bottle around the first and join the top edges together with paper clips. You should now have four cylinders, one at each corner. Make sure the moulds are square with each other and with the foundations. Tape along the inside joins of the two bottle halves. Strengthen the outside of each mould with further strips of tape. Now check that each mould is approximately 80 mm in diameter. The towers need to be cast 180 mm high, so mark this level on the inside of each mould. Seal the outer base edge of each mould with Plasticine.

So that you do not use excessive amounts of plaster, glue a 30 mm × 30 mm strip of polystyrene to the foundations inside each mould. Make sure this filler strip clears the walls of the mould.

Do not attempt to cast a tower in one go as the weight of liquid plaster will burst the mould. The trick is

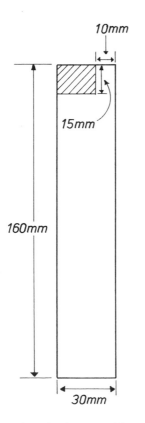

10mm

15mm

160mm

30mm

Fig. 4.5 Cross-section of polystyrene slab used for castle wall, showing wall walk.

to fill the bottom of each mould with about 10 mm of liquid plaster of paris. Allow this to set for 15 minutes, before carefully filling the mould with further applications of liquid plaster.

Fill to the 180 mm mark and allow the castings to set for a couple of hours before removing the moulds.

The four towers on the gatehouse are cast in exactly the same way. Their dimensions are: the two towers facing the inner ward, 200 mm high × 55 mm diameter, the twin towers facing the outer ward, 190 mm high × 70 mm diameter. You will find that one washing-up-liquid bottle will suffice for each mould.

Making the curtain wall

The wall connecting the four towers around the inner ward, is called the curtain wall. It is made from 30 mm thick polystyrene, or from two or three thinner sheets glued together to make up the right thickness. Figure 4.5 shows a cross-section of the wall, with provision for a wall walk and ramparts at the top. As the distance between the towers will vary, you must measure the distances yourself. Aim to make the side walls and the back wall first. These should be fixed to the towers and foundations with a general purpose filler.

The approximate sizes for the four walls of the gatehouse, are shown in figures 4.6 to 4.8. Note that there are no wall walks cut into these and that the side walls sit flush with the top of the front two towers. Fix the gatehouse walls in place with general purpose filler, before measuring the two curtain walls which join the gatehouse to the front corner towers.

Moulded inner corners of curtain wall

A glance at figure 4.1 will show that the inner corners of the curtain wall curve in around the four corner towers. Make cardboard moulds to fit along the corner outlines which should still remain on the foundations. The inside of the card should be lightly coated with Vaseline, before the pieces are taped into place. Seal the bottoms of the moulds, before casting.

Final tower castings

The height of the two inner facing towers of the gatehouse, will now need to be extended by a further 60 mm. Tape a washing-up-liquid bottle around the top of each tower. Seal as before and cast with plaster of paris.

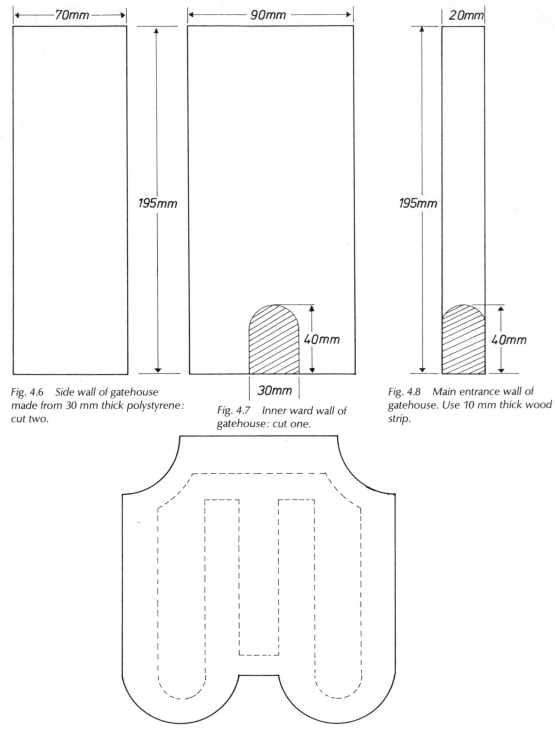

Fig. 4.6 Side wall of gatehouse made from 30 mm thick polystyrene: cut two.

Fig. 4.7 Inner ward wall of gatehouse: cut one.

Fig. 4.8 Main entrance wall of gatehouse. Use 10 mm thick wood strip.

Fig. 4.9 Gatehouse roof: cut from the template card C.

Completed model of the castle. Ramparts on the main towers have been modelled from quick drying clay. The model is now ready for painting.

The two corner towers at the rear of the castle, each have a smaller tower built onto the curtain wall corner sections you have just cast. These additional towers measure 80 mm high × 40 mm diameter. Cast these from smaller plastic bottles.

Gatehouse roof

Cut the gatehouse roof shape shown in figure 4.9 from the template. The area within the broken lines denotes the leaded roofed section, which should be painted lead-grey. The guttering area around the lead roof should be painted stone colour. Glue the roof in place over the gatehouse structure.

Ramparts on towers and gatehouse

There are two ways in which you can make the ramparts around the towers and gatehouse. You can cast them, which will provide a cleaner finish. Or you

can model them from self-hardening clay. Craft shops and model shops have a variety of clays of this nature. In the model of Harlech Castle shown in this book, all the tower ramparts were modelled from clay, except for the two smaller rear watch-towers which were cast from plaster of paris.

To cast from plaster, tape a plastic strip around each tower top. This strip should be wide enough to give a casting depth of 20 mm. Place a smaller plastic or card cylinder inside the first mould. Cover inside walls of mould with Vaseline. There should be a 10 mm gap between the walls. Cast from plaster of paris. When set, the castellation can be cut to a depth of 15 mm with 10 mm spacing. Use a razor saw or a junior hacksaw to cut down the edges of the pieces to be removed, then carefully chip away the gap with a craft knife.

If you are moulding the ramparts from clay, remember that the clay will shrink a little on

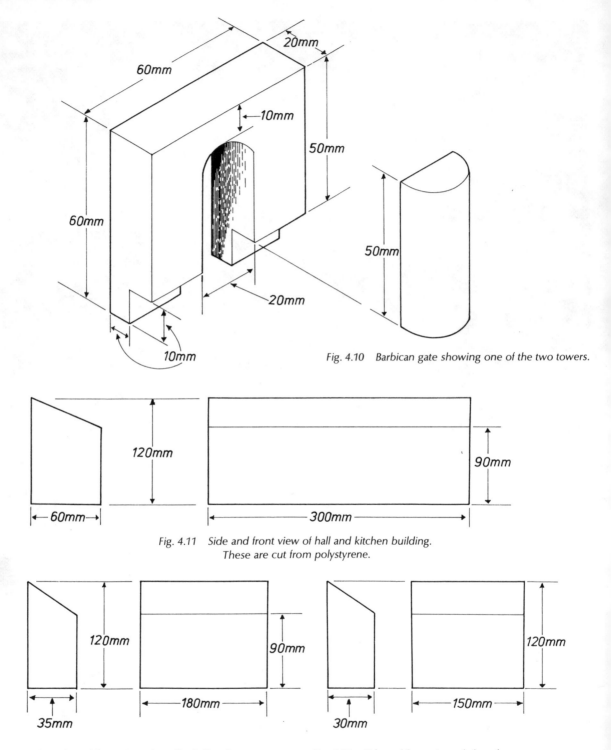

Fig. 4.10   Barbican gate showing one of the two towers.

Fig. 4.11   Side and front view of hall and kitchen building.
These are cut from polystyrene.

Fig. 4.12   Side and front view of smaller hall and granary.   Fig. 4.13   Side and front view of chapel.

hardening. Allow a little extra on the following dimensions.

Roll, flatten and cut the clay into strips 270 mm long × 20 mm wide × 10 mm thick. Check that the strips will fit around the sections you are working on. Place the strip flat on a piece of board. Place a ruler 15 mm in from one of the 270 mm long edges and cut out the castellations with a knife. Shape the cut out clay and fit onto each tower. Allow to harden. A resin glue will fix the dried clay sections to the towers and gatehouse.

The ramparts around the curtain wall and the outer ward, should now be cut out with a craft knife. Make these 15 mm deep with 10 mm spacing.

Barbican gate

The barbican gate is made from a piece of balsawood cut into an arch, see figure 4.10. The diagram also shows one of two barbican towers, these should be made from 20 mm diameter dowel. Each piece of dowel should have a 5 mm thick strip shaved off it with a knife. This flat area will allow the tower to be fixed to the barbican gate. Cement the finished structure to the model with general purpose filler.

Inner buildings

The buildings within the inner ward are made from slabs of polystyrene. Figure 4.11 shows the great hall and kitchen buildings, which are glued to the inner side of the back curtain wall. Figure 4.12 shows the smaller hall and granary, which are fixed to the inner side of the left wall. The chapel is shown in figure 4.13 and is set against the inner side of the right wall.

Roofs, for the inner buildings, can be made from card cut from the remainder of the template. Small steps leading to the great hall and to the front of the barbican gate can be modelled from clay.

Finishing off the model

The inner ward can be coated with sand, see the section *Ground texture* in Chapter 3.

Use poster paint for this model, as other paints will probably eat into the polystyrene. The castle should be painted a stone colour, with the roof sections painted a lead-grey. Landscaping around the model can be painted earth-brown, with patches of rock-grey and lichen-green.

5 Oakworth Station

Oakworth Station is one of five stations owned and run by The Keighley and Worth Valley Light Railway Ltd., on a line from Keighley to Oxenhope. The line is situated in West Yorkshire and a good part of its fame must be attributed to Haworth Station, which serves the town where the Bronte sisters were born. The formation of the original company in the 1860s, was prompted by The Midland Railway Company opening an extension line from Leeds and Bradford to Keighley. The prime objective of the local company was to service the transport needs of local worsted mills dotted along the proposed route. It was also envisaged that, as soon as the line opened, freestone and slate would be quarried.

From the beginning The Keighley and Worth Valley Light Railway Ltd. had strong links with The Midland Railway Company who agreed to run the line on its completion. The engineers responsible for the lines construction were Mr J S Crossley, engineer to The Midland Railway Company and Mr John McLandsborough, a local man who undertook most of the detailed work. In 1866 the track was completed and a test run was arranged for November 1866. Travelling on the first train were Mr McLandsborough and three of his clerks, the contractor and his sons, a Midland porter and the Keighley stationmaster. It took the train about two hours to cover just under five miles of track, as frequent stops had to be made to remove debris from the line. The return journey was made in 13 minutes. The line was a success from the start, its prosperity helped by the wealth of the worsted industry and a growing local population. Many additions and improvements were made to the line over the years, and it was at its peak in the period prior to the first world war. Evidence of this can be seen from the records, which show that a large number of working people used the line daily. Parcel delivery was a full time job and twenty-four hour manning was called for in the signal boxes. Up to five thousand ton of coal a week was handled by Haworth Station and each week countless van loads of cloth were transported to Bradford.

From 1918 onwards the line began to lose its goods to road transportation. This decline continued until 30 December 1961 when the last regular passenger train made its way along the four and three-quarter miles of track.

The line was neglected until March 1962 when The Keighley and Worth Valley Preservation Society was formed. Their principal aim was to preserve the Worth Valley Railway and this they have done.

Oakworth Station has, as near as possible, been restored to its appearance in 1900 when the line was in its heyday. The station was used for location shots in the film *The Railway Children* and was instrumental in providing an authentic background.

My model of Oakworth Station has been designed to 4 mm scale, 00 gauge. For the most part, the model utilises ready made plastic sheeting and fittings, both of which are available from modelling shops. The station is designed to be free standing or to fit into an intended layout. Those of you wishing to construct the entire line as a layout, can obtain a route map and gradient profile from,

The Keighley and Worth Valley Light Railway Ltd.,
Haworth Station,
Haworth,
Keighley,
West Yorkshire.

You will need

– the following tools

Hand saw.
Small craft saw or junior hacksaw.
Craft knife and spare blades.
Metric ruler, preferably steel.
Carpenter's square or set square.
Compasses.
Drill and bits.
Artist's brushes.
Scissors.
Small domestic sieve.

– the following materials

One piece of softwood, 1194 mm × 150 mm × 16 mm, for the base.
Two sheets of embossed plastic 00 gauge dressed stone, 250 mm × 300 mm, about five course of stone to every 10 mm.
Two sheets of embossed plastic undressed stone, 250 mm × 300 mm, approximately two courses per 5 mm.
One sheet of plain white plastic about the thickness of a greeting card.
One sheet of plain white plastic, 1.5 mm thick.
One sheet of transparent acetate for window glass.

Two sheets of embossed plastic, 00 gauge stone flagging, 250 mm × 300 mm.
One sheet of embossed plastic, 00 gauge cobbles, 250 mm × 300 mm.
Small quantity of 4 mm plywood offcuts.
Eight strips of plastic angle, 300 mm × 2 mm × 2 mm.
Two strips of round plastic tubing, 300 mm × 2 mm diameter.
Several matchsticks and wooden lollipopsticks.
1 m of 00 gauge fencing, including two small gates and one large gate.
Seven freestanding 4 mm gas lamps with square glass.
One sheet of 00 gauge signs and posters.
String and wire for making trees, or purchase three ready made trees from a model shop.
Small bag of gravel chippings and fine sandstone soil.
One bottle of Plastic Weld.
Small tube of PVA glue.
Tin of impact adhesive.
Tin of yellow stone, G W R Stone no. 1, matt paint.
Tin of dirty-black paint, deep grey in colour, matt finish.
Tin of matt white paint.
Tin of cream paint, gloss.
Tin of deep brown paint, gloss.
All the above paints are best purchased from a model shop in 50 cc tins or smaller.

To begin your model

Mark out the base

The base is made from a piece of softwood, which should be planed and rough sanded. Figure 5.1 shows a plan of the baseboard. The front edge is shown in figure 5.2. Notice the cutaway ramps at each end of the platform, these stretch back to the horizontal broken dotted line. The curve on the left side of the platform front should be formed by glasspapering after the baseboard has been cut.

The broken lines on figure 5.1 denote the positions of the station buildings. Transfer these lines to the baseboard before cutting any of the pieces.

Flagging and cobbling the base

The front edge of the platform and the inner edges of the siding should be covered with undressed stone embossed plastic sheet. Use impact adhesive to fix the sheets in place, making sure to sand a 'tooth' into the back of the plastic before applying the adhesive. Use a ruler and craft knife to cut the sheeting taking care to achieve good joins between the various lengths of plastic. The siding should be capped around its upper face with 4 mm wide strips of undressed stone.

The platform front and the station house area should now be covered with stone flagging. Strips of 2 mm plastic angle should be welded along the edge of each piece of flagging where the flagging meets the platform edge. To do this, cut the flagstone sheet to size and tape a piece of 2 mm plastic angle along one edge of the sheet. Brush a little Plastic Weld along the join and allow to dry for a few seconds. Remove the tape. The welded edge can be lightly sanded to disguise the join. Now fix the plastic angle in place over the platform edge. Use impact adhesive. The flagstone edge lines at the edge of the platform can now be cut into the strip of plastic angle. Except for the area behind the siding, the remaining area of the base should be covered with cobble pattern. The area behind the siding will be covered with stone chippings.

The bare sections at the back of each ramp should be given a dressed stone effect by covering the walls so formed with 00 gauge dressed stone plastic sheet. Remember to cap the top of these two walls with one course of stone.

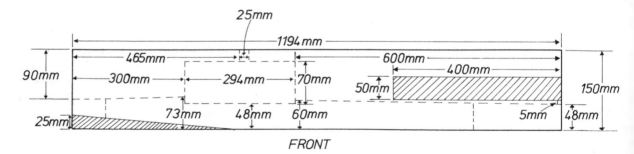

Fig. 5.1 Baseboard.

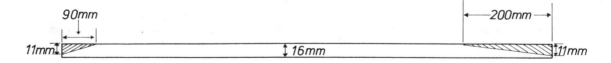

Fig. 5.2 Front view of baseboard; notice the cut-away slope at the front of the platform (shaded area).

Constructing the station house

Fig. 5.3   Layout showing position of walls. Front faces platform.

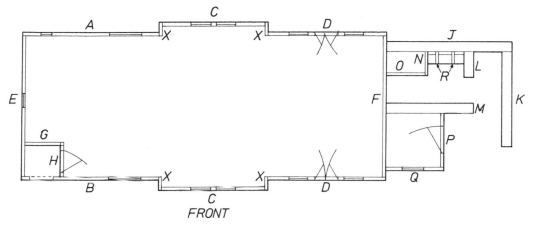

Applying plastic strips to the window frames of the C pieces. This builds up the appearance of wall thickness. The strip is held with Plasticine while it is welded to one side of the frame. The strip is then slowly bent and welded around the frame.

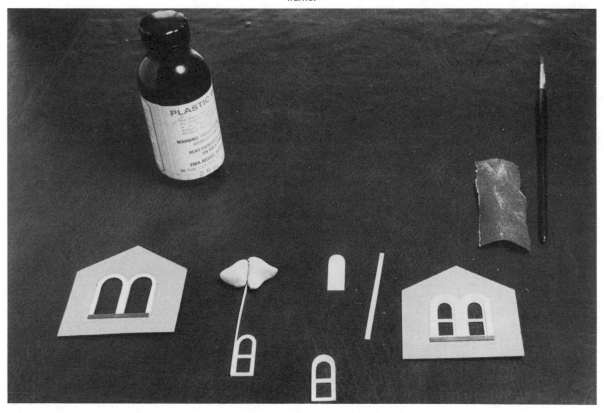

The station house is constructed from sheets of embossed plastic 00 gauge dressed stone. Refer to figures 5.4 to 5.12. Each piece is lettered according to its position in the plan of the station buildings, see figure 5.3. Cut one of A, four of X, one of B, two of C and D, one of E, F, G and H. The broken lines above the windows and doors denote the position of the lintels. These lintels are 2 mm in depth and overlap the side edges of the windows and doors by 1 mm. Carefully cut out the lintels, reverse them and push them back into the space on the sheet. Weld them along the edges. The broken lines in figure 5.8 denote areas where a further thickness of dressed stone sheet should be welded in place. This is needed to achieve the recessed effect of the stone work on pieces D.

Now refer to figure 5.13 which shows how the lintels and wall thicknesses are built up around each window. Notice how the top window lintel, 2 mm plastic angle, is welded onto the reverse side of the plastic, while the bottom lintel, 2 mm plastic angle, slips through the bottom window edge from the front. Strips of dressed stone plastic sheet are then welded to strips of 2 mm plastic angle, which are welded along the inner sides of the windows. The same technique is also applied to the door openings, except that the bottom lintel is omitted.

A slightly different technique of wall thickening is applied to pieces C and D. Take one of the C pieces and place it on top of a piece of thin white plastic sheet. Draw a line around the inner edges of the windows and remove the C piece. Draw a second line 2 mm out from the first line. The area between the two lines is the dressed stone window surround. Cut the surround from the sheet of white plastic and fix it above the bottom lintel on the outside of piece C. Do this for both pieces. The same method should be used to make the arched surrounds on pieces D, but note that these fit *above* the two windows and doorway. The white window shaped blanks of plastic sheet that were left over from the surrounds in pieces C can be utilised for the window frames. Make the thickness of each frame 1.5 mm. You will also need window frames for the D pieces. To achieve the appearance of wall thickness around the windows, 2 mm wide strips of plastic sheet should be welded around the window frames before the window frames are welded to the window spaces on pieces C and D.

Pieces of the main building completed and ready for assembly. The bottom row is shown in reverse.

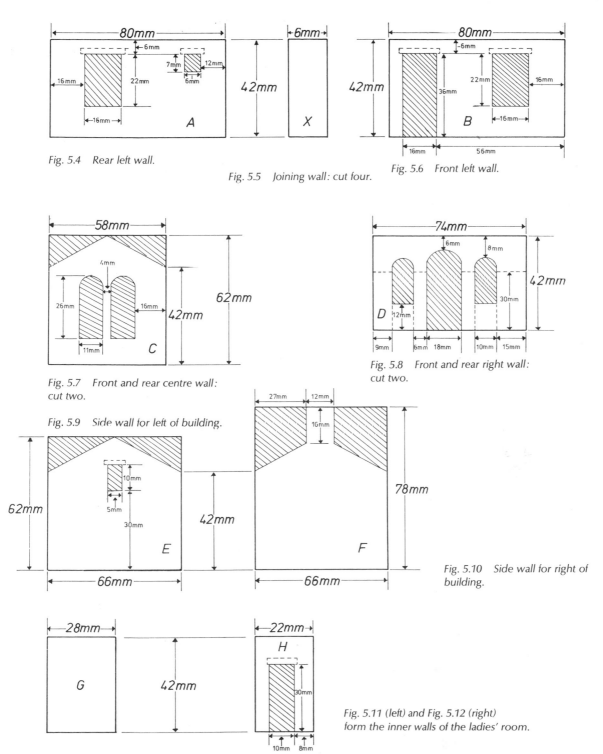

Fig. 5.4   Rear left wall.

Fig. 5.5   Joining wall: cut four.

Fig. 5.6   Front left wall.

Fig. 5.7   Front and rear centre wall:
cut two.

Fig. 5.8   Front and rear right wall:
cut two.

Fig. 5.9   Side wall for left of building.

Fig. 5.10   Side wall for right of
building.

Fig. 5.11 (left) and Fig. 5.12 (right)
form the inner walls of the ladies' room.

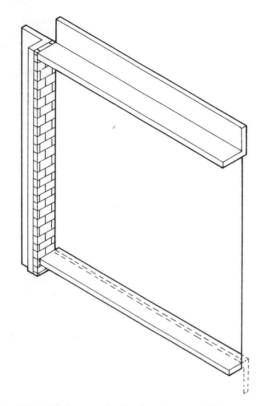

Fig. 5.13 *Building up the lintels and stone thicknesses around the windows.*

The wall thicknesses around the doorways in pieces D should be made from 2 mm wide, 60 mm long strips of dressed stone plastic. These are welded around the inner edges of the doorways. Window frames for pieces A, B and E, should be made in the way just described.

Before assembling station building, paint the window frames with deep brown gloss. You should also paint the white plastic window surrounds a lighter shade than the surrounding brickwork. The colour for this can be made by mixing one part matt white to three parts matt stone colour paint. The dressed stonework around the windows and doors and pieces G and H should be painted yellow stone. When the paint work has dried, cut the window glazing from a sheet of clear acetate. The borders around the window-panes should be painted on the acetate sheet in light cream gloss. Weld the glazing in place behind the window frames.

Assembling the building

Weld a length of 2 mm plastic angle to the side edges and bottom edges of pieces E and F. Note that plastic angle should always be welded on the inside of the building pieces.

Refer to figure 5.3 which shows how each piece overlaps and joins. Weld A and B to E, using the plastic angles already welded to the side edges of E. Weld the D pieces to F.

Using plastic angle, weld two X pieces to each C piece.

Now weld the structure E–A–B to the flagstone area on the base. When looked at from the platform, E should have its outside bottom edge level with the line between the cobbles and the flagstones on the left of the building area. Piece A should be about 6 mm from the line between the cobbles and the flagstones at the rear. Using further angles, weld G and H into position.

Weld the two C–X structures to pieces A and B and to the base.

Check that everything is square before continuing. Should you need to reposition any of the pieces, soften the joints with Plastic Weld and pull apart. Complete this stage by welding structure F–D to pieces X and to the base.

The door to piece H, the ladies' room, and the doors to pieces D should now be cut from plain plastic sheet and welded in place. Figure 5.26 shows the ladies' room door, paint the black area with deep brown gloss. Figure 5.27 shows the pattern for the doors to pieces D. Paint the black area with deep brown gloss, the white spaces being painted with light cream gloss.

Before roofing, paint the flagstones inside the building. The flagstone colour should be mixed from one part stone colour to one part dirty-black matt paint.

Gutters and stone dressing

The gutters for pieces A and B are made from 2 mm plastic angle. Cut the plastic angle so it sticks out 2 mm past piece E. Weld one edge of the plastic angle to the wall so that the other edge juts up parallel to the wall, the top of the plastic angle being level with the top of the wall. Stop the open end of the gutter with a small square of plastic.

The gutters for pieces D are 5 mm wide cut from plain plastic, 1.5 mm thick, see figure 5.14. Each gutter

Welding the pieces together. 2 mm plastic angle is used to fix the walls to each other and to the base.

Welding the left roof flats in position. Notice the gutters, and the way the appearance of roof thickness is made.

Fig. 5.14   Gutter for D piece: cut two.

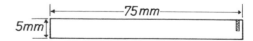

has a slot sawn 1 mm from one end, this allows it to slot over the sloping edges of *F*. These gutters should be rested flat on top of the wall and welded in place with a 1 mm overlap on the outside face of pieces *D*.

Roofing

Using figure 5.18 cut out two roof pieces for the C walls. Dressed stone sheet was used for this model. The stone dressing and moulding is made from thin plain plastic sheet and from 1.5 mm thick plastic sheet. Figure 5.15 shows how this is assembled. Note how a thin roof support sheet fits under the thick dressing strip.

Taking one roof piece at a time weld the roof pieces to the supports on the C pieces. Check that all is square.

Figure 5.16 shows the size of the two roof flats that slope down towards A and B. Figure 5.17 shows the two roof flats for the opposite end of the building.

To achieve the effect of tile thickness and to add finishing boards to the end of the roof, weld thin plastic strips to the end of each flat, see figure 5.19. You should cut an angle at the end of each strip where it will meet the gutters. Note that only one 2 mm wide strip is required on each of the flats in figure 5.17. In this case, the flats should have a slot cut in the top corner, to fit around the chimney section of F.

Weld the roof flats in place to the building, making sure the ridges are central.

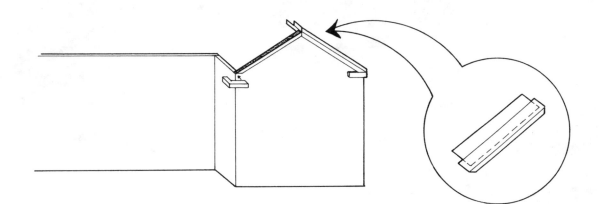

Fig. 5.15   Stone dressing attached to roof support sheet. Centre walls.

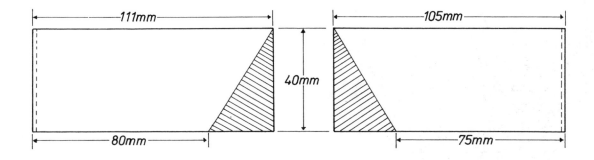

Fig. 5.16 (left) and Fig. 5.17 (right)   Roof flats: cut two of each.

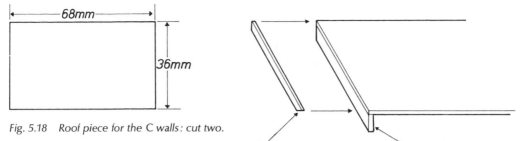

Fig. 5.18 Roof piece for the C walls: cut two.

2mm wide strip   4mm wide strip

Fig. 5.19 Building up tile thickness.

Chimneys

The two chimneys are cut from blocks of balsa or softwood. The side and end view of the chimney to the left of the building is shown in figure 5.20. Figure 5.21 shows the side and end view of the chimney to the right end of the building. Note that the right-hand chimney glues to the inner face of the chimney section of piece F, figure 5.10. The bare wood chimneys are now clad with dressed stone plastic sheet. When this cladding is dry, each chimney base should be dressed with plain plastic sheet, the broken lines on figures 5.20 and 5.21 show the positions for this.

Cap the top of each chimney stack with a rectangle of plain plastic. The chimney pots can be made from matchsticks, or from 2 mm diameter plastic tubing. Make each chimney pot 6 mm long and fix it into a thick layer of adhesive applied to the chimney capping. This layer of adhesive can later be painted to look like mortar.

2 mm plastic tubing, split along its length, can be used for the roof ridge. Cut the tube into 30 mm lengths before splitting along the length with a ruler and knife. Score a tile effect along each resultant strip, then weld the strips to the roof ridges.

The effect of lead flashing, where the roof sections join, can be made from 3 mm wide strips of plain paper, glued along the lines in the roof.

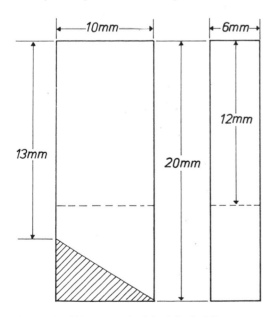

Fig. 5.20 Chimney to the left of the building.

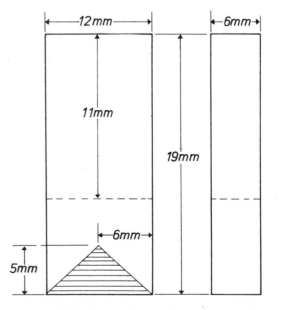

Fig. 5.21 Chimney attaches to chimney section of F.

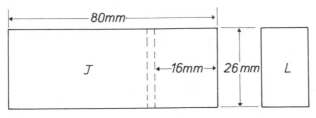

Fig. 5.22 (left) and Fig. 5.23 (centre) show the back wall of w.c. L attaches to the broken lines, at a right angle to J.

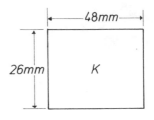

Fig. 5.24 Side wall of w.c. unit.

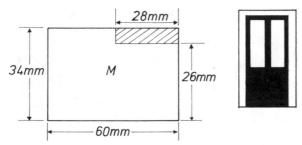

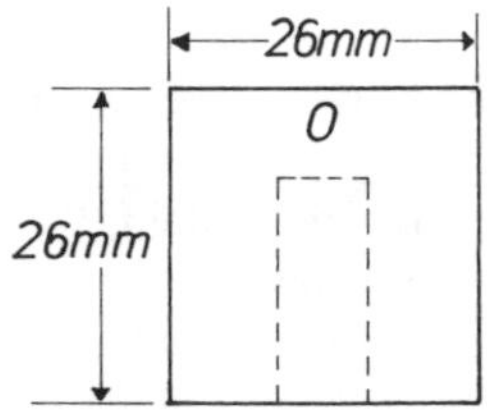

Fig. 5.25 (left)   Rear wall of porters' room.

Fig. 5.26 (centre left)   Door for porters' room and ladies' room: cut one for each.

Fig. 5.27 (centre right)   Door for piece D: make two.

Fig. 5.28 (right)   Front wall of w.c.

Porter's room and w.c.

The porters' room with the mens w.c. and urinal behind it, is sited at the right-hand end of the main building. Pieces J, K, L and M, figures 5.22 to 5.25 are cut out of 4 mm thick plywood. Make sure the edges of the plywood are square after cutting.

Take piece J and using contact adhesive fix the edge of piece L to the position indicated by the broken lines in figure 5.22. See also figure 5.3. J and L should now be fixed to the main building and to the base with contact adhesive. J should be on a line 3 mm from the rear right-hand corner of the main building. Piece M is positioned 18 mm from, and parallel with, the inner face of J. M's longer side of 34 mm being fixed to the main building. K is fixed at right angles to the outer end of J, refer to figure 5.3.

The bare surface of pieces J, K, L and M can now be covered with dressed stone plastic sheet. When glued in place the top edges of the plastic sheet should be level with the top edges of the plywood. Realism can be added to the urinal area by covering the bottom half of J, the innerside of J, with plain white plastic sheet.

Paint the wall pieces yellow stone. Pieces O and N, shown in figures 5.28 and 5.29 make the w.c. Piece O can have a door set into it, but this will hardly be visible when the model is assembled. O and N should be made from dressed stone sheet and welded into the position shown in figure 5.3. Paint both pieces stone colour. Note the piece N slips over the wall created by J.

90

The porters' room and w.c. area. The roofs will be put in place once the plywood has been capped with plain plastic strip.

The porters' room is assembled from dressed stone plastic sheet. The design is shown in figures 5.30 and 5.31. Assembly is the same as for the w.c. except that a door needs to be incorporated in piece *P*. Gutters for the porters' room can be made from 2 mm plastic angle or from 2 mm diameter tubing.

Before roofing, add two pieces of plain plastic sheet, 5 mm × 15 mm. These form *R*, the urinals in figure 5.3. One section of sloping roof is fixed over the w.c., figure 5.32, and two sections over the porters' room, figure 5.33. The roofs should have their thickness built up at one end with narrow strips of plastic sheet. Use the method you used for the roof sections of the main building.

Finally, cap the surrounding walls with strips of 1.5 mm thick plain plastic sheet.

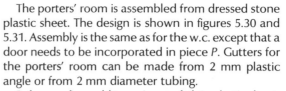

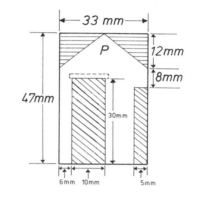

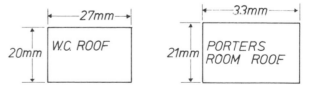

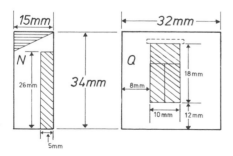

Fig. 5.29   Side wall of w.c.

Fig. 5.30   Front wall of porters' room.

Fig. 5.31 (top)   Side wall of porters' room.

Fig. 5.32 (left)

Fig. 5.33 (right)

The completed station building seen from the track side. Notice the fencing and the lamps.

Fencing

Early advertising plates fixed to the fencing are a feature of Oakworth Station. You can buy a sheet of 00 gauge paper advertising plates from a model shop.

Using ready made 00 gauge fencing, which has been painted light cream gloss, weld the fencing to the line formed where the flagstones meet the cobblestones. As the fencing comes in short strips, its assembly is an easy affair. Glue the advertising posters to each strip before welding it in position. Put a small gate against the left-hand corner of the building and a medium gate near the w.c. wall, *K* in figure 5.3.

Lamps

Gas light station lamps can be bought from a model shop. These are usually made of metal, with a clear plastic glass. The glass should have four sides. Mount three lamps on the left side of the platform and two lamps on the right side. Paint the stem of the lamps with light cream gloss and paint the crossbars with deep brown gloss. Small holes need to be drilled to take the bases of the lamps. A further lamp can be mounted, minus its stand, to the station building. Using a piece of wire, fix the lamp to the right end of the gable above wall *C*.

Station sign

The station sign is made from plastic sheet and

Fig. 5.34   Station sign.

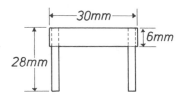

matchsticks. Figure 5.34 shows the dimensions of one sign, you will need to make two, one for each end of the station. The sign background is deep brown gloss, the letters are in light cream.

Trees

Small bushy trees can be purchased from a model shop. You will need three or four of these to line the back of the fencing to the left of the station. Drill small holes to fix the trees to the base.

Landscaping

The bare wood area behind the siding, can now be covered with 00 gauge chippings. But, before you do this, you might like to add a small station yard crane. This should be fixed to plastic sheet slabs, which

Rear view of the completed building.

Oakworth Station built to 4 mm scale and ready for use.

should be fixed to the bare wood.

Coat the wood with PVA glue and, using a domestic sieve, sprinkle the glue with fine sand. Overlap the cobbles and around the siding. While this is drying, sprinkle small amounts of fine sand around the back and sides of the building and under the trees.

When dry, brush off the surplus sand. Coat the sand behind the siding with PVA glue before applying the chippings.

Finishing off

Roofs should be painted dirty-black. The stone work should be painted yellow stone, with the lighter stone colour, mixed earlier, used for lintels and stone dressing. To achieve a weathering effect, mix the stone colour with a small quantity of dirty-black. Using an almost dry brush, rub this colour over the dry painted surface of the building. You will find that the brick work is picked out and the walls begin to look realistic. Matt white should be used along the edge of the platform. Paint, matt white, one course of stone around the base of the station building.

Working Notes

Working Notes

Working Notes